GROWING SLOWLY WISE

BUILDING A FAITH THAT WORKS

DAVID ROPER

MDF PUBLISHING

Unless otherwise indicated, Scripture is taken from the HOLY BIBLE, NEW
INTERNATIONAL VERSION, copyright © 1973, 1978, 1984 by Biblica, Inc.™ Used by
permission of Zondervan. All rights reserved.

Scripture quotations which are the personal translation of the author are based on the
Greek edition *Novum Testamentum Graece*, Nestle-Aland edition (NA28).

You can read more from the author at http://davidroper.blogspot.com/

Cover photo: Little Redfish Lake in the Sawtooth Mountains of Idaho. One of the
author's favourite locations. Photo by Joshua Roper, Joshua Roper Photography.
https://www.joshuaroperphotography.com/

ISBN 978-1-7776615-3-3 (print - non-Amazon edition); 978-1-7776615-5-7 (print -
Amazon edition); 978-1-7776615-4-0 (e-book)

Published by MOF Publishing; mofpublishing@proinbox.com; mofpublishing.com

MOF PUBLISHING

Some months ago I received a letter from a man that read the chapter I entitle "Wising Up" when it first appeared as an "E-Musing"—a series of short essays I send to a few friends.[1] I don't know the man personally, but I know the tangle he's made of his life. He wrote the following:

I have read carefully your work on wisdom.... I am trying to come to grips with the implications of what I have done and work through to the end what I have to do to achieve that "gentle wisdom." This episode in my life has reminded me of (Wagner's) characterization of Parsifal: "the good man slowly wise." The "slowly" seems very slow indeed. But with God's gift of each new day, I will pursue it to the end.

Hence the title: *Growing Slowly Wise.*

CONTENTS

INTRODUCTION

"If the Epistle is 'of straw' then there is within that straw a very
hearty firm, nourishing, but as yet uninterpreted and unthreshed
grain."

—Johann Gottfried Herder

Martin Luther had a hard time with James' book. He thought it
utterly bereft of God's grace, a throwback to the law and order days
of the Old Covenant. He could see no indication that James understood Paul's great themes of justification and sanctification by faith
that had so powerfully influenced his conversion. And so he gave
the book scant attention, calling it, "an epistle of straw." "James," he
wrote, "is a very dangerous and bad book...I feel like throwing
Jimmy into the stove."

Later, I'm happy to say, Luther, whose great mind was always growing, revised his opinion of James' book, perhaps as a result of discus-
sions with his colleague Philip Melanchthon and after reading John
Calvin's commentary on James, and surely as a result of the
prompting of the Holy Spirit. "I think highly of James (now)," he
wrote, "and regard it as valuable...."

I too have a hard time with James' book, but for a different reason. I too think highly of it and regard it as valuable, but it's a hard read, not because it's hard to understand—indeed, I understand it too well —but because it is full of what Jesus' early disciples would have called "hard sayings," precepts that are hard to hear. Indeed, James steps all over my toes; I can't read his book without flinching.

He looks into my heart and sees bottomless evil—pride, prejudice, self-righteousness, hypocrisy and deceit. He targets my cold, deliberate sins of the spirit and delivers his message with lethal accuracy. As Howard Hendricks used to say, "James doesn't strafe the deck; he drops the bomb right down the funnel."

James segues rapidly from one searching concept to another in what we would call today "a stream of consciousness," touching on a subject, illuminating it, expanding it, applying it and then moving to another thought, triggered by an idea that associates itself in his mind. His arguments are not always easy to follow since he gives us few grammatical markers to show us how his mind is working.

Despite James' somewhat distracting tendency to shuttle readily from one topic to another, however, there is one clear theme that warps its way through the woof of his writing. It is that good, old-fashioned word, holiness. James would have us "holy as God is holy."

Holiness is a dull word these days, conjuring up images of fusty, finger-wagging prigs, who are good in the worst sense of the word, men and women with sullen, morose faces, full of rectitude and rigid duty, "on hold for the next life," as a Washington Post writer once put it.

True holiness, however, is anything but dull. It is startling and arresting. It is more than being decent, good, ethical and upright. It has that aspect the Bible calls "the *beauty* of holiness." It is what Paul has in mind when he calls on us to "*adorn* the gospel" (Titus 2:10).

Likewise Peter, writes, "Live such good lives among unbelievers that, though they accuse you of doing wrong, they may see your good deeds and glorify God on the day he visits us" (1 Peter 2:12). The word, here twice–translated "good," means "something beautiful to see."

This is the picture of holiness James draws for us, a portrayal that fascinates us, and awakens us to the hope that we can be more than we ever hoped to be; that we too can live lives of uncommon beauty and grace. It can happen as we humbly receive it. "The LORD...will beautify the humble," Israel's poet assures us (Psalms 149:4).

This is also the picture of holiness that can fascinate our unbelieving friends and awaken in them the hope that there may, after all, be something more.

Most people long for truth and righteousness though that desire is often frustrated by what they see in certain Christians, whom they perceive as self–righteous, rigid, loveless, humorless folks who never crack a smile, who can't abide a joke, whose "virtues are too numerous to describe, and not sufficiently interesting to deserve description," as Anthony Trolope said of his qualmish Miss Thorne, whose odd–ball behavior only puts them off. Such "virtue" is far less interesting to unbelievers than vice with the result that they cling to their vices though they may hate them. They are overthrown not by the devil, but by the Christians they know. Joy Davidman puts a fine point on it when she writes, "One sanctimonious (Christian) makes a hundred unbelievers."

Sad to say, few have seen the real thing—that extraordinary quality of life of which James speaks, which can only be described as "beautiful." Would that you and I had it. "If only 10% of the world's population (did)," C. S. Lewis once mused, "would not the world be converted and happy before a year's end?"

David Roper

Boise, Idaho 2021; http://davidroper.blogspot.com/

JAMES—A SERVANT OF THE LORD

"The forcible writer stands boldly behind his words
with his experience. He does not make books out of
books, but he has been *there* in person."

—Henry David Thoreau, *Journal* March 18, 1842.

JAMES, A SERVANT OF GOD AND OF THE LORD JESUS CHRIST, TO THE
twelve tribes scattered among the nations: Greetings (James 1:1).

If I were James I would have introduced myself as, "James, the
brother of Jesus," for that's exactly who he was. The Gospel writers
affirm it (Matthew 13:55; Mark 6:3), and Eusebius, the 4th century
"Father of Church History," confirms their witness: "Then there was
James, who was known as the brother of the Lord; for he too was
called Joseph's son...."

Furthermore, I would have presented my credentials, for James was
a distinguished and celebrated leader in the early church. According

to Eusebius, the Apostles, shortly before they were scattered by Saul's persecution, "chose James the Righteous as Bishop of Jerusalem." Luke, in the book of Acts describes James in that role, guiding the church in Jerusalem through her formative stages with profound wisdom and practical insight. On one occasion, at the first gathering of church leaders with certain Apostles present, it was James' opinion, rather than the Apostles', that had the greater weight (Acts 15:1–29).

Yet James, resisting the impulse to pull rank and drop the Name, in the "humility that comes from wisdom," describes himself merely as, "a servant of God and of the Lord Jesus Christ." James was a simple, modest man.

Humility is hard to come by these days. More than we care to admit it, many of us in leadership are in it for the recognition, the accolades, the personal honors and prestige the positions bestow on us. Indeed, how many occupations offer so many opportunities to look good, to gain glory, to be deferred to, to be admired, to show how wise and knowledgeable we are? We casually mention our education, our degrees, our academic accomplishments, our publications, hoping to impress others with our knowledge and relevance and thus have greater influence. Yet, ironically, it's that posturing that strips us of real influence—our ability to influence others toward God.

Humble, simple people have always been the best mentors. They don't seek to be great. They don't grandstand, nor do they draw attention to themselves. They don't "lord it over those entrusted to them, but serve as examples." They look honestly at their own weaknesses and their own need for forgiveness and therefore they're gentle, patient and forgiving when others fall short and fail. They're tractable, teachable and thus more knowledgeable. We learn from them because, like Jesus, they're "meek and lowly in heart."

Charles de Foucauld's words from long ago remain apropos: "Never think that in lowering yourself you have less power for good. On the contrary, in thus humbling yourself you are imitating and using the same means that I (Jesus) used. You are walking in my way and therefore in the truth, and you are in the right state to receive life and impart it to others. The best means for this is my way. I came down to the level of men by my Incarnation and to that of sinners by my Circumcision and Baptism. Be lowly, lowly, lowly, humble, humble. Let those that are in high places put themselves last in a spirit of lowliness and service, love for men, humility, taking the lowest place so long as the divine will does not call you to another, for in that case you must obey... If you are placed high, then keep yourself in humility of soul as though you were last; occupy your high position as though you were there only to serve others and to lead them to salvation" (Meditations of a Hermit).

There's another thing about James: he rang true. Eusebius again, quoting another early historian, Hegesippus, described James as one whom "everyone from the Lord's time till our own has called 'The Righteous One,'" using a word for righteous that means, "as one *ought* to be." Like Chaucer's parson, James was an "example for to give, by his purity, how that his sheep should live." He taught...

Christ's lore, and his Apostles twelve,
He taught, but first he followed it himself.

Obedience is essential for teachers because it is the basis of spiritual insight and understanding. George MacDonald wrote: "What (the biblical writers) care about is plain enough to the true heart, however it is far from plain to the man whose desire to understand goes ahead of his obedience.... He who does that which he sees, shall understand; he who is set upon understanding rather than doing, shall go on stumbling and mistaking and speaking foolishness. It is he that runneth that shall read, and no other."

Furthermore, obedience is necessary because it is the foundation of all spiritual power. Authority is not won by education, personality, intellect, experience or promotion, but by a will to obey. Even Jesus said, "If I do not do my Father's deeds don't believe me" (John 10:37).

It's foolish to be heedless of our own inner life while instructing and giving counsel to others. "Take heed to *yourself*," said Paul, and (then) to your teaching."

There's a third factor that invites me to learn from James: he was willing to suffer for what he believed. He understood there is no ministry without misery, no proclamation without pain, no renewal without the possibly of retaliation. He had what ancient Christians called *habitus practicus*.

Habitus practicus, as you might guess, is an old Latin phrase that suggests the habit of proclaiming the truth without fear or favoritism and a willingness to suffer the consequences of that proclamation. It's something of a lost art these days, yet it lies at the heart of every call to ministry.

Habitus practicus is seen in Moses' putting up with a grumbling, ungrateful people for forty years; in Jeremiah's emotional pain as he confronted the malicious, lying prophets of Israel; in Stephen's ministry and martyrdom; in Paul's oft–repeated description of the sufferings he bore for the sake of the Gospel; in Jesus' exhortation to all disciples to live as "sheep among wolves"; in his invitation to discipleship: "If anyone would come after me, he must deny himself and take up his cross and follow Me." It's seen in James' readiness to die for what he believed.

Jewish historian, Josephus, tells us that shortly after the death of Festus, the governor of Judea, the high priest, Ananias, who hated and opposed James, convened a kangaroo court, charged James with violations of the Law and stirred up the citizens of Jerusalem to kill him. Eusebius gives this account of James' final days:

> When Paul appealed to Caesar and was sent to Rome by
> Festus, the Jews were disappointed of the hope in which they

had devised their plot against him and turned their attention to James the Lord's brother... This is the crime they committed against him. They brought him into their midst and in the presence of the whole populace demanded a denial of his belief in Christ. But when, contrary to all expectation, he showed undreamed of fearlessness in the face of the enormous throng...they could not endure his testimony any longer, since he was universally regarded as the most righteous of men. So they killed him.

Eusebius then quotes Hegesippus, who may have interviewed eyewitnesses to the event:

When many even of the ruling class believed, there was an uproar among the Jews and Scribes and Pharisees, who said there was a danger that the entire people would expect Jesus as the Christ. So they collected and said to James: "Be good enough to restrain the people, for they have gone astray after Jesus in the belief that he is the Christ. Be good enough to make the facts about Jesus dear to all who come for the Passover Day. We all accept what you say: we can vouch for it, and so can all the people, that you are a righteous man and take no one at his face value. So make it clear to the crowd that they must not go astray as regards Jesus: the whole people and all of us accept what you say. So take your stand on the Temple parapet, so that from that height you may be easily seen, and your words audible to the whole people." For because of the Passover all the tribes have forgathered, and the Gentiles too.

So the Scribes and Pharisees made James stand on the Sanctuary parapet and shouted to him: "Righteous one...tell us what is meant by 'the door of Jesus.' He replied as loudly as he could: "I tell you, the Son of Man is sitting in heaven at the right hand of the Great Power, and He will come on the clouds of heaven."

Many were convinced, and gloried in James's testimony, crying, "Hosanna to the Son of David!" Then again the Scribes and Pharisees said to each other: "We made a bad mistake in affording such testimony to Jesus. We had better go up and throw him down, so that they will be frightened and not believe him."

So they went up and threw down the Righteous one. Then they said to each other "Let us stone James the Righteous," and began to stone him, for in spite of his fall he was still alive. But he turned and knelt, uttering the words: "I beseech Thee, Lord God and Father, forgive them; they do not know what they are doing."

While they pelted him with stones, one of the descendants of Rechab, the son of Rachabim, the priestly family to which Jeremiah the Prophet bore witness, called out: "Stop! What are you doing? The Righteous one is praying for you."

Then one of them, a fuller, took the club which he used to beat out the clothes, and brought it down on the head of the Righteous one. Such was his martyrdom. He was buried on the spot, by the Sanctuary, and his headstone is still there by the Sanctuary.

One mark of integrity is a willingness to go to the wall for what one believes. James went all the way

Finally, I'm drawn to James because he makes sense: he speaks to those instinctive and essential truths that enable us as human beings to associate with one another in kindness, courtesy, faithfulness, love and delight. Coleridge called it "common sense to an uncommon degree." James calls it "wisdom."

James method is not so much to inform as to restate the obvious, for no one has to tell us what we ought to be. We know. We cannot in fact rid ourselves of these intuitions, and our desire to conform ourselves to them. The problem, as it has always been, is compliance.

So James calls to mind those behaviors that are good, true and beautiful, and then, in the simplest way possible, tells us how to do them. He writes in a homely fashion, appealing to the heart of the average man or woman, boy or girl. He talks sense and makes it accessible to all.

There's an old Yiddish word, *mensch* that like so many Yiddish words says it all. A *mensch*, according to my Yiddish dictionary, is "someone who is true, sensible, wise enough to be no longer naïve, but not cynical; a person who gives advice for our benefit rather than his or her own. A *mensch* acts not out of fear, or out of a desire to make a good impression, but out of strong inner conviction of who he or she is and what he or she stands for. A *mensch* is whole," or, as the biblical writers would say, "complete."

James is my *mensch*.

2 SUFFERING SUCCESSFULLY

May all your expectations be frustrated;
May all your plans be thwarted
May all your desires be withered into nothingness...
That you may experience the poverty of a child
and sing and dance in the compassion of God
Who is Father, Son, and Spirit. Amen.

—A blessing from Larry Hine, Brennan Manning's spiritual director, delivered as the benediction at Manning's ordination service

CONSIDER IT PURE JOY, MY BROTHERS, WHENEVER YOU FACE TRIALS OF many kinds, because you know that the testing of your faith develops perseverance. Perseverance must finish its work so that you may be mature and complete, not lacking anything (James 1:2-4).

"I would like to say something about God's purpose for pain," C.S. Lewis wrote, "but I have a terrible toothache this morning." I feel the same way this morning, writing as I am with a torn rotator cuff and struggling to work through the pain.

Pain is real, as pleasure is real. Sickness, loneliness, humiliation, frustration, solicitation to sin—"trials of many kinds"—fall on us like bricks tumbling out of a dump truck, one after another. "If anything *can* go wrong, it *will* go wrong" Murphy's Law assures us, and, as a beleaguered friend of mine once observed, Murphy was an optimist.

Yet there is another law—James' Dictum, I call it: "Suffering Matures Us." Pain, far from being an obstacle to our spiritual growth and development, is the condition of it, the means by which we gain the final graces and virtues for which we yearn and for which we have long prayed. It is the story of every man or woman who has marked his or her age. It is the way we become "mature and complete." Without it we would never make the most of our lives.

James defines our trials as "the testing of (our) faith." The word "testing" means "tested and *approved*." The word is found on the bottoms of ancient clay vessels that had been formed, fired, inspected and found flawless. (It served the same purpose as our "Good Housekeeping Seal of Approval.")

"Faith," the other word James uses, is reliance on God and on his resources to see us through the solicitations, vagaries and exigencies of this world. It is more than mere belief; it is a steady determination that by God's indwelling presence and power we will turn what we believe into godly behavior. Suffering is the means by which that perfect end is accomplished. Here's how it works:

When trouble comes we have two options. We can view it as an intrusion, an outrage, or we can see it as an opportunity to respond to it in specific obedience to God's will. This is that rugged virtue James calls, "endurance."

Endurance is not tooth-clenched resignation, nor is it passive acquiescence. It is "a long obedience in the same direction." It is staying on the path of obedience despite counter-indications. It is a dogged determination to pursue holiness when the conditions of holiness are not favorable. It is a choice in the midst of our suffering to do what God has asked us to do, whatever it is and for as long he asks us to do it. As Oswald Chambers wrote, "To choose suffering makes no sense at all; *to choose God's will in the midst of our suffering makes all the sense in the world.*"

We won't always choose to do what's right. There will be times that we forget God's Word, his enabling grace, or simply refuse to do his will. There's something in us so flawed and fallen that it will not rise to the occasion. Nevertheless, as soon as we can, we must get back on the path of obedience.

I think that's what James means when he prompts us to let perseverance "have its perfect result." We must keep on keeping on. We must join with God in the work of maturing us. We must persevere till the perfecting work is done. The only *fatal* flaw, as C. S. Lewis said, is to give up.

We're inclined to fret while we're in process, impatient with our progress, wondering if God knows what he's doing, restless that he has not removed our sorrow, wanting to give up, getting sour inside and feeling sorry for ourselves.

"I wonder why God made me," grumbles Mrs. Faber, one of George McDonald's characters, her sad heart worn out by long–suffering. "I'm sure I don't know what was the use of making me." "Perhaps not much yet," replies her friend, Dorothy, "but then He hasn't done with you yet. He is making you now, and you are quarreling with the process."

God is making us now; we're only half–done. But he is at work using every contrivance—even pain—to do it. We must not quarrel with the process, but bear our share of suffering, not striving anxiously to do our best, but looking into each sorrow for its lesson and into God's Word to find the corresponding act of obedience that the occasion requires, then asking God for his will and way to obey.

If only we would believe that we're in–process and under way and willingly consent to be made. If only we would submit fully to our Maker's hands as the clay submits to the potter. If only we would yield to the turning circumstances of his wheel. If only... If only... We would soon be able to welcome the pressure of that hand—even when it's felt in pain—and see the end in view, the bringing of one of God's sons unto glory.

I read recently these words from Isaiah: "For you, O God, tested us; you refined us like silver. You brought us into prison and laid burdens on our backs. You let men ride over our heads; we went through fire and water, but you brought us to a place of abundance" (Psalms 66:10-12).

Silver is tested by fire but the heart is tested by pain. The main thing in life is not to do, but to become. For this we're being prepared every day.

It's hard to understand why year after year some hard ordeal is perpetuated. It seems like our time is wasted; we're doing nothing and therefore nothing is being done. What we must see is that behind every difficulty lies the purpose and love of God. We have been placed in the particular set of circumstances that will give us the best opportunity to manifest and thus acquire those virtues in which we are most deficient. A hard marriage, a difficult child, a meaningless occupation, a lingering illness, confining old age—all these hardships have been screened through God's love for our good.

He sits patiently beside the crucible, intent on the process, tempering the heat, skimming away the scum, waiting until his face is perfectly reflected in the surface.

Nothing can happen to us that has not first passed through God's hands. "Not a single shaft can hit/Till the God of love sees fit." We'll not be destroyed, God assures us. Only what is unworthy in us will be burned away. We can rest in God's will and see what he will make of us in the end.

Knowing that God is behind our suffering makes it much more meaningful. "The will of God is like a soft pillow," F. B. Meyer said, "upon which I can lie down and find rest in all circumstances."

Our ordeal may be a call to be very bold in the face of great opposition, or to stay sweet in the presence of prolonged aggravation. Whatever—God is with us. He will send us grace to obey for as long as we need it. Every day a new strength and courage will come into us and we will be able to do or endure a little more than we ever thought possible. We will find ourselves becoming stronger, better, wiser. Perseverance is doing its perfecting work, gradually turning us into the kind of man or woman we now most admire.

If you fail today, don't worry. You're a fully forgiven child of God, on the way to perfection. Someday you'll stand before him, "having no spot or wrinkle," and God will say to his Son, as he said of his first creation, "That's *beautiful*! Just what I had in mind all along!"

And in the meantime, though you suffer great pain, you will be comforted and loved. Paul wrote, "Praise be to the God and Father of our Lord Jesus Christ, the Father of compassion and the God of all comfort, who comforts us in all our troubles..." (2 Corinthians 1:3-5).

Some years ago National Public Radio carried an interview with Madeline L'Engle, in which she spoke at length of the relationship between faith and imagination. She ended with this story that comes from the Jewish rabbinical tradition: "A student came to a rabbi and asked, 'In Isaiah why is God's word written *on* their hearts instead of being *in* their hearts?' The rabbi answered, 'They are not yet ready for that. It is on their hearts so that when their hearts are broken the word might fall in.'"

God's word comes to us in the brokenness of our health, in the disintegration of our personalities, in the severing of our marriages, in the crumbling of our friendships, and in the shards of our dreams. It surrounds us waiting for the smallest break by which it may enter in.

Therefore, "consider it pure joy whenever you face trials of many kinds." Cheer up! Sing! Rejoice! God is making of you a better thing than you ever thought possible.

> *Our master craftsman ceases not with skillful hands of love*
> *To weave our life to that of Christ sat glorified above;*
> *And though first, like a quilt work, as seen from underneath,*
> *If patient till the final threads we see his finished piece.*
>
> *It takes the threads of silver, of gold and brighter hue,*
> *But also one's of red and black to make a picture true.*
> *Whom else but God knows when and where to put each tiny stitch;*
> *Just when to try and when to bless to work a pattern rich*
>
> *And though his word is sure and firm that all things work for good.*
> *We fear those pricks that bring the cords, transforming frames of wood.*
> *So yield your empty frame of wood, hewn out from Calvary's tree*
> *And let each moment from henceforth be worked as he would see.*

—Unknown

James would have agreed.

3

WISING UP

"To deviate from the truth can never be wise…
The wisest course for the disciple is always to abide
solely by the Word of God in all simplicity."

—Dietrich Bonhoeffer

BUT IF ANY OF YOU LACKS WISDOM, LET HIM ASK OF GOD, WHO GIVES TO all men generously and without reproach, and it will be given to him. But let him ask in faith without any doubting, for the one who doubts is like the surf of the sea driven and tossed by the wind. For let not that man expect that he will receive anything from the Lord, being a double-minded man, unstable in all his ways (James 1:5-8).

We long to be "mature and complete not lacking *anything*" (James 1:4), yet we find ourselves to be such fools, especially in times of discomfort and trouble. God, however, suffers fools gladly. We can ask for wisdom when we need it and it will be given "generously and without reproach," as James puts it. "God gives without twitting (taunting us for embarrassing mistakes)," was John Bunyan's quaint, but dead–on translation of James' promise.

It's important, however, to know what wisdom is, for it's not what we *know*—we can make that acquisition on our own—but what we ought to *be* and, according to James, that accumulation is well beyond us. It comes from above.

Jesus' Beatitudes offer deep insight into what it means to be wise. He spoke of *being* pure, *being* humble, *being* merciful. He spoke of attitudes and virtues that are deep within us, and said, "If you want to be happy and wise this is what you must *be*."

Theologian Fenton Hort, in like manner, describes wisdom as, "that endowment of heart and mind which is needed for the good conduct of life." Wisdom is "right conduct," but it is more than merely being good. (God save us from good people!) It is God's gift of rare beauty to our souls—what the scriptures call "the beauty of holiness"—and it always looks best against the dark background of deep suffering.

And what does wisdom look like? Well, for starters (and only for starters) it is reasonable, flexible, forgiving, peaceful, caring, given to friendly visits, small acts of courtesy and kind words. It doesn't look sagacious or pious. It is humble, transparent, simple, gentle, gracious to the core. Wisdom, as Solomon would say, softens our face (Ecclesiastes 8:1).

"Where can wisdom be found?," Job asked in his shattering sorrow, "It cannot be found in the land of the living. The deep says, 'It is not in me'; the sea says, 'It is not with me.' It cannot be bought with the finest gold, nor can its price be weighed in silver. It cannot be bought with the gold of Ophir, with precious onyx or sapphires. Neither gold nor crystal can compare with it, nor can it be had for jewels of gold. Coral and jasper are not worthy of mention; the price of wisdom is beyond rubies. The topaz of Cush cannot compare with it; it cannot be bought with pure gold. "Where then does wisdom come from?"

Then Job answers his own question: "God understands the way to it and he alone knows where it dwells" (Job 28:12, 23).

Wisdom is beyond the reach of human determination. It is not in us or around us. It "comes from heaven," as James will later affirm (James 3:17). We must "ask" for wisdom. Then and only then can it be given. "Wisdom," wrote Spurgeon, "is a beauty of life that can only be produced by God's workmanship in us."

God is not satisfied to save us from this world alone. He wants to change us, to make us real in the righteousness that is in his Son. The only path to real change is to ask for his help. When we do, we're in for the full treatment. God's goal for us is greater than we could ever imagine.

However, there is a proviso: when we ask, we must "believe and not doubt." Here "doubt" has nothing to do with honest questions of faith, but with being "double-minded" or "two-souled," to use James' exact word—wanting holiness, but not wanting it, if you know what I mean.

The two-souled person is divided, unsure if he wants to do what God has asked him to do. This is John Milton's, "Mr. Facing Both Ways." This is young Augustine and his bifurcating, delaying prayer: "Lord, make me pure—but not yet." This is the man or woman on the fence, who, James assures us, "should not think he will receive anything from the Lord." He is like "a wave of the sea, blown and tossed by the wind...." He is "unstable in all he does"— erratic, fearful, restless, clueless, useless.

Jesus prayed at the moment of *his* greatest trial, "Not my will, but yours be done." In the midst of our troubles, when we ask for the wisdom of God's will we must, like our Lord, be willing to do it. Only then can the gift be given. As George McDonald put it so well, "God will carry us in his arms until we can walk, and he will carry us when we cannot walk. But he will not carry us in his arms if we *will* not walk."

I have to ask myself from time to time, "Am I wising up as I grow older, or am I just getting to be another old fool?" Aging can make us bitter and mean–spirited, or, by God's grace it can make us more gracious. So much depends on the way we're growing.

Life is relentlessly dynamic. We're either growing sweeter and easier to get along with, or we're growing into sour–faced old curmudgeons whom no one can stand to be around. (They call it "going bad" in Narnia.) Orneriness is one of the crowning works of the devil. The question is always this: which way am *I* growing?

Despite our sinful folly God loves us with an ardent, intense affection that can deliver us if only we will yield ourselves to him. His love can make the most difficult nature into a miracle of astonishing beauty. It may hurt a little and it may take awhile—we grow "slowly wise," as Wagner's Percival said—but God seeks at last our transformation. Wisdom will begin to rise in us and pour itself out to others.

Here is James' promise: when trials beset us and we lack wisdom— when we're tempted to fall into meanness, moodiness, ill–temper, bitterness and other bad behavior—we can ask for wisdom and "it will be given...." If, in the midst of our troubles, we ask for God's help he will hear us.

"Wisdom cries out," said the Wise Man: "Let all who are *foolish* come in here!" (Proverbs 9:4). Wisdom has only one qualification: we must know that we're great fools.

4

THE POOR RICH AND THE RICH POOR

"I have more than E. H. Harriman (the railroad magnate),
for I have all the money I want, and he hasn't."

—John Muir

But let the brother of humble circumstances glory in his high
position; and let the rich man glory in his humiliation, because like
flowering grass he will pass away. For the sun rises with a scorching
wind, and withers the grass; and its flower falls off, and the beauty
of its appearance is destroyed; so too the rich man in the midst of his
pursuits will fade away (James 1:9-11).

Once upon a time, as most apocryphal stories go, there was an
investment counselor who encountered a genie on the way to the
office. When granted a wish he asked for a copy of *US. News and
World Report* one year hence and hurriedly turned to the market page
to plan his killing.

He got more than he bargained for, however. There on the opposite page he spied his own face—in an obituary describing his death in an automobile accident the previous day.

That's the trouble with money, you know: *we* go. "The sun rises with scorching heat and withers the plant; its blossom falls and its beauty is destroyed. In the same way, the rich man will fade away even while he goes about his business" (James 1:10,11).

The brevity and flimsiness of life have inspired numerous metaphors in literature: human existence is compared to a dream, a flying shuttle, a mist, a puff of smoke, a shadow, a gesture in the air, a sentence written in the sand. Here James compares our life span to a spray of flowers that wither and die in the wind.

We spoil our entire lives trying to accumulate money. We ruin our vacations, health, marriages, children, and friendships—and for what? In the end we wither and die and leave our wealth behind. That's why money is such a bad investment.

There's more to money, however, than the fact that we leave it behind. The greater problem is that it can ruin our lives right now. It makes us believe that money, when we have enough of it, will make us secure and significant.

Jacob Needleman, writes in the introduction to his book, *Money and the Meaning of Life,* "I have always pictured poverty as associated with fear and anxiety about the future, fear of abandonment, fear of physical danger, and fear of loneliness. I see the poor as trapped, tense, cunning, harsh. I see them bored, empty of hope, or consumed by absurd fantasies...." The answer, he goes on to say, is to make money, for money talks and tells us we're very significant.

Money does talk, as Needleman insists, but mostly it lies to us. It really isn't true that money will make us feel successful and secure. The well–heeled know it isn't true: enough is never enough. Having money is just a goad to get more.

Furthermore, money also deceives us by telling us we're wise and powerful. As Tevya, the fiddler on the roof, mused, when you got rich it doesn't matter if you answer right or wrong, "cause when you're rich they think you really know." But, isn't it odd that rich men, stripped of their wealth, are often considered great fools?

Financial ruin can make you look foolish, but it can also be an occasion to gain great wisdom. It teaches us James' odd inversion: "The brother in humble circumstances ought to take pride in his *high* position; the one who is rich should take pride in his *low* position" (James 1:9,10).

Poverty can enrich us because in it we learn the secret of true wealth. Being rich isn't about money, you see; it's a state of mind. There is a wealth that leaves us poverty–stricken and a poverty that makes us fabulously rich.

Money, if we love it, will impoverish us for it will turn our hearts from good. "If your eyes are bad," Jesus said, "your whole body will be full of darkness. If then the light within you is darkness, how great is that darkness!"(Matthew 6:22,23).

If we fix our eyes on Mammon it will darken our hearts, cloud our judgments and leave us morally confused and uncertain. It will lead us into bad decisions—choices that defy logic and cause us to deny our highest values. We will fudge, cheat, embezzle, misappropriate, pad and pilfer. We will, in the end, do *anything* to make a buck. The light in our heart will go out and, as Jesus said, "How great is that darkness!" (Matthew 6:23).

But worse, the love of money will turn our hearts from God. "No one can serve two masters," Jesus said. "Either he will hate the one and love the other, or he will be devoted to the one and despise the other. You *cannot* serve God and Money" (Matthew 6:24). If we think about money all the time we will, in time, take no thought of God.

Mammon destroys our natural appetite for God. It substitutes one hunger for another. We're taken up with fashion, style, vogue, decor;

we transfer our taste from primary to secondary things and God fades from our minds. Wanting money, what wise men call greed, is a state of mind in which it's easier to forget God than any other.

John Bunyan, in his Pilgrim's Progress writes of the ruin of some travelers: "Now on the far side of that plain was a little hill called Lucre and in that hill (there was) a silver mine, which some of them, because of the rarity of it, had turned aside to see. But going too near the brim of the pit the ground being deceitful under them broke and they were slain. Some also had been maimed there, and could not to their dying day be their own men again."

If we love money that devotion will inexorably supplant our passion for God and we will be maimed and slain by it. We will be "devoted to the one" and will "despise the other." We may dabble with God for a time, but in the end we will deny him. "One master–passion in the breast…swallows up the rest," said Alexander Pope.

So—God in his mercy will do one of two things for us: he will give us money and leave us with heart–breaking disappointment in it, or he will take it all away. Either way, God is at work, humbling us, ridding us of our preoccupation with Mammon, loosening our grip on "earth's toys and lesser joys" as my Carolyn says, setting our affection on things above. This is the ruin that enriches us; the "low position" that leaves us better than ever before.

What God leaves behind is pure gold: we have God and all that he gives. We need nothing more. Israel's poet wrote out of his poverty, "I am always with you; you hold me by my right hand. You guide me with your counsel, and afterwards you will take me into glory…. Whom have I in heaven but you and earth has nothing I desire besides you…. As for me, it is good to be near God" (Psalm 73:23–28).

This is the good life; this is the richest man in the world!

5

WHY COMES TEMPTATION?

Why comes temptation but for man to meet
And master and make crouch beneath his feet,
And so be pedestaled in triumph?

—Robert Browning

BLESSED IS THE MAN WHO PERSEVERES UNDER TRIAL[1], BECAUSE WHEN HE has stood the test, he will receive the crown of life that God has promised to those who love him. When tempted, no one should say, "God is tempting me." For God cannot be tempted by evil, nor does he tempt anyone; but each one is tempted when, by his own evil desire, he is dragged away and enticed. Then, after desire has conceived, it gives birth to sin; and sin, when it is full-grown, gives birth to death. Don't be deceived, my dear brothers. Every good and perfect gift is from above, coming down from the Father of the heavenly lights, who does not change like shifting shadows. He chose to give us birth through the word of truth, that we might be a kind of firstfruits of all he created (James 1:12-18).

. . .

Life is temptation. It pursues us through childhood, adolescence, adulthood, old age and senility—right up to the gates of heaven. It entices us at work and play. It intrudes into our thoughts, our dreams, and even into our prayers. "Temptations to sin are *sure* to come," Jesus said.

God could spare us from such enticement, but he has determined not to do so—for good reason: "God permits temptation to sin," said Augustine, "to transform it into greater good."

"Bad people, in one sense, know very little about badness," C. S, Lewis said. "They have lived a sheltered life by always giving in. We never find out the strength of the evil impulse within us until we try to fight it...."

Temptation makes us aware of "the strength of the evil impulse within us," and reveals the fragile stuff of which we're made. It humbles us. It makes us more reliant on God's strength, and therefore less likely to yield.

James goes so far as to say we are "blessed" by temptation (the same word found in Jesus' Beatitudes) for when we have persevered (resisted temptation) we will receive the "crown of life." James uses a word for crown that in his day referred to the olive wreath given to those who competed in the games and ran well. The crown of life is a winner's crown given to one who has run life's race, finished strong and is "pedestaled in triumph."

Though God allows temptation he is not the source of it, James assures us. "When tempted, no one should say, 'God is tempting me.' For God cannot be tempted by evil, nor does he tempt anyone" (James 1:13).

It is not in God's nature to draw us into sin. No, *we* are the problem. We are tempted when we are "dragged away and enticed" by our *own* desires—our longings for something other than God, or something more than God has chosen to give us.

Sin begins with provocation—a bare thought, an enticement to evil. So long as the provocation is image–free—is not allowed to become imagination and fantasy—there is no sin. Temptation only becomes sin when we imagine the act and linger with great pleasure over the images. The old Christian writers called this "coupling," because at this point we've joined our minds and emotions to sin.

Then the will is engaged—we assent to sin's urges and act upon them—which in turn predisposes us to habitual and continuous sin. In principle we retain our free will, but in practice the force of habit makes it more and more difficult to resist and leads us into obsessions, compulsions, frustration, depression and a deep weariness that has no cure. This is how temptation "gives birth to sin; and sin, when it is full-grown, gives birth to (soul) death."

Later, James will tell us of another dynamic at work: an evil personality behind all temptation, our adversary the devil who "baits" us, to use James' exact word, hooks us and draws us into sin (James 4:7).

Jesus described the devil as a "liar and a murderer" (John 8:44), a devious, homicidal maniac akin to Dr. Hannibal Lecter, the psychiatrist turned psychopathic killer in *The Silence of the Lambs*. Lecter was called "Hannibal the Cannibal," because he ate his victims. Satan likewise is skulking about, "looking for someone to devour" (1 Peter 5:8). He is a predator always on the prowl, hungry for flesh, and we are his prey.

Like most psychopaths, however, Satan is suave and charming. "He hath power to assume a pleasing shape," Hamlet said. He is a gentleman with civil manners and impeccable taste. He was high–born and therefore can insinuate himself into good company. He surrounds himself with beautiful people and makes their behavior— even deviant and dangerous acts—look good to us. We read about their life–styles and "eat it up," as we say, not knowing that *we* are the ones who are about to be consumed. Satan is up to no good.

God, on the other hand, is up to nothing but good, and has nothing but good in store for us: "Every good and perfect gift is from above, coming down from the Father of the heavenly lights, who does not change like shifting shadows." He is the creator of light—all that is good and true and beautiful—and the one who gives us light. There are no shadows or darkness in him, no double–dealing, no deceit, no duplicity. He is pure truth.

By means of truth God "chose to give us birth…that we might be a kind of first fruits of all he created" (James 1:18). This is another way of saying that God's purposes are wholly good. In contrast to Satan who wants to take life, God longs to give it. The "word of truth" is the means by which life was originally given and the means by which it is sustained and brought to completion. Through truth we become God's "first–fruits"—the cream of the crop, the crème de la crème, the very best that a man or woman can be.

How, then, can we avoid being taken in by Satan's menace and deceit? *By taking heed to God's word.* Here's how it works.

Satan's proposals always begin with a feint, a false lead, a lie, some subtle twist to the truth, which, if acted upon, would tear us away from God, and, if followed to the end, would terminate us. His proposals rarely seem evil—our minds are repelled by obvious evil —more often they come under the guise of good. Satan adds a tincture of grace and beauty to every lure lest we recognize its lethal toxicity. It's very easy to be taken in.

We must meet every one of Satan's lies with truth—meet it when it first enters our minds. Thomas à Kempis said, "Temptations are more easily overcome if they are never allowed to enter. Meet them at the door as soon as they knock, and do not let them in.

The way to fend off Satan is to meet him at the beginning before he gathers strength and overwhelms you. Be vigilant, watchful alert. Meet him immediately with a word from God and banish him, as you would dismiss some obnoxious traveling salesman, before he gets his foot in the door. Remind yourself of some word that God has given you that speaks to the particular lie Satan is advancing and submit yourself to that truth.

That was our Lord's response to the devil's temptations. Satan's strategy was to taunt Jesus into disobedience, but with each assault, our Lord seized upon a specific text: "It is written...." In each case he countered Satan's deceit with a corresponding truth and humbly submitted himself to it.

That's what James calls "perseverance"—a dogged determination to pursue holiness when the conditions of holiness are not favorable. It is resisting the devil by recalling what God has asked you to do and determining by his grace to do it. It is the way to overcome the evil one. "One little word," says Luther, "will fell him."

I'm reminded of a *Far Side* cartoon I saw some years ago, depicting a woolly mammoth lying on its side dropped by a tiny arrow. Two awe–stricken cave men stand side–by–side with bows in their hands, gaping at what they had done. "We've got to remember that spot," one says to the other.

Satan has a soft, unprotected underbelly: he is vulnerable to God's Word. To that end we must give ourselves to knowing it, hiding it in our hearts (Psalm 119:11); meditating on it day and night (Psalm 1: 2); allowing it to "dwell in (us) richly" (Colossians 3:16). Satan's power lies in deceit; our weapon is truth. "Our defense is sure."

According to Homer's Odyssey, Odysseus was trying to get home to his family and was having a hard time doing it. Along the way he encountered the enchanting and dangerous Circe who, it was said, turned men into pigs.

When Odysseus successfully avoided her attractions, she confided in him that sterner tests lay ahead—the Sirens, lusty, luscious maidens whose island lay along the straits and whose songs lured travelers away from hearth and home.

Circe advised Odysseus to have his men plug their ears with wax and tie himself to the mast. Odysseus, however, had another, better idea. He did have his men plug their ears and he did tie himself to a mast, but he also had his friend Orpheus, who was also an accomplished musician, sit on the deck and make a melody so sweet it would turn his heart away from the Sirens. In that way he "stood the test." He stayed his narrow course and made it home to his beloved Penelope.

So, when Satan begins to croon one of his alluring, fatal tunes, sing to yourself the lyrics of God's Word, "sing and make music in your heart to the Lord" (Ephesians 5:19). And then submit yourself to that Word. This is Paul's "way of escape" (1 Corinthians 10:13). It's the only way to get through.

6

THE LAW THAT SETS YOU FREE

"Obedience is the road to Freedom."

—C. S. Lewis

MY DEAR BROTHERS, TAKE NOTE OF THIS: EVERYONE SHOULD BE QUICK TO listen, slow to speak and slow to become angry, for man's anger does not bring about the righteous life that God desires. Therefore, get rid of all moral filth and the evil that is so prevalent, and humbly accept the Word planted in you, which can save you. Do not merely listen to the Word, and so deceive yourselves. Do what it says. Anyone who listens to the Word but does not do what it says is like a man who looks at his face in a mirror and, after looking at himself, goes away and immediately forgets what he looks like. But the man who looks intently into the perfect law that gives freedom, and continues to do this, not forgetting what he has heard, but doing it—he will be blessed in what he does (James 1:19-25).

· · ·

James has written of the "word of truth," our sure defense against the devil. This, he continues, "you know."[1] But it's not enough to merely know the Word. We must "listen (to it)" and "do what it says."

Here James enjoins the necessity of response. The difference made by the Word is the difference it makes in us, but for it to make any difference at all, we must decide whether we will receive it with humility, or place ourselves in opposition to it.

The point James makes is complementary to Jesus' parable of the sower and the seeds (Matthew 13:1–9). The seed is the Word that is "planted" in us. It comes to us through reading, through preaching and teaching and the counsel of wise friends. If we are good soil it will implant itself in us, take root and eventually bear fruit. If we do not receive the Word it will go some other place and find root in someone else, happily producing the fruit of the Spirit. We will, however, have disturbed ourselves and become very unsound— angry and full of neurotic aggression.

The word James uses, translated "angry," suggests an ambient (in contrast to transient) anger. Archbishop Richard Trench defines it as "a settled habit of mind." It is deep–seated hostility and bitterness of soul, a restless, argumentative spirit that inveighs against our right- eousness, the goal to which this book is directed.

Odd isn't it, that when we will not "do" the Word—when we see our sin mirrored on its pages and walk away defiant, unrepentant—we degenerate into resentment against God and his people. That's because there is no moral stasis. We're either becoming more gentle and gracious, or more warped and embittered. There is, as philoso- phers say, no *tertium quid* —third thing.

The way to grow in grace is to be "quick to listen"[2]—to hear what God is saying to us. That's an idea James sets in contrast to being "slow to speak (talk)," i.e., chatter on about God's Word—analyzing it, dissecting it, abstracting it, all the while building walls of pride and reason so the heart can remain independent. "Saying and not doing," as you may know, is one of James' dominant themes.

James is concerned here with our tendency to approach the Bible as an object of intellectual curiosity—to study it assiduously, to talk about it incessantly, but do nothing with the data we collect. This James says, is like looking into a mirror and seeing dirt on our faces, but choosing to do nothing about it. We believe the word, but we do not think in terms of repentance, faith and obedience. Such reading, James insists, is downright dangerous.

C. S. Lewis has this sort of person in mind when he has his senior demon, Screwtape, give the following advice to his nephew, Wormwood:

> The great thing is to prevent his (Wormwood's new Christian client) doing anything. As long as he does not convert it into action, it does not matter how much he thinks about this new repentance. Let the little brute wallow in it. Let him, if he has any bent that way, write a book about it; that is often an excellent way of sterilizing the seeds which the Enemy plants in a human soul. Let him do anything but act. No amount of piety in his imagination and affections will harm us if we can keep it out of his will.

The problem is that the more we keep the Word out of our will the more theoretical, abstract and distant God becomes. Then terrible things begin to happen to us: our hearts begin to harden (because unlived truth always brutalizes us), coldness sets in and eventually bitterness overwrites our souls.

Truth does call for some discussion and understanding, but not as much as we think. There is an order in the way God reveals truth and that order is inviolate: he speaks; we obey; he explains—maybe.

It is simply not true that we must understand a text before we can obey it. God is not obligated to explain anything to us and there are some things he will never be able to explain until we get to heaven and have his pure heart. We must obey whether we understand or not. We must put an end to our garrulous, restless, quibbling about God's Word and "humbly accept" it.

James' word, "humbly," is a great Greek word with no exact English equivalent. It refers to one who is teachable, tractable, modest enough to take counsel and learn. It is one who is willing to bow before each word in humble submission. As T. S. Eliot put it,

> You are not here to verify,
> Instruct yourself, or inform curiosity
> Or carry report. You are here to kneel.

Note James' order: we must rid ourselves of "all moral filth and evil." "Moral filth" is anything that is dirty and that defiles us as human beings. (The word meant "ear wax" in ancient medical textbooks.) "Evil" is a generic term for anything ugly and demeaning that "entwines itself" (the meaning of "prevalent") around our souls and entangles us.

James is not insisting that we set ourselves right before the Word can set us right. That would be tautology. No, James is concerned here with a *disposition*, a fundamental willingness to put off anything that defiles us, body, soul or spirit.

What James means is this: if we find ourselves reading the Word and unchanged by it, it may be that there is some *unwillingness* in us to let God repair everything that is unworthy or wrong. Unreadiness and resistance tie his hands.

What is the solution? To "humbly accept the Word," to drop our defensive posture, to read with a readiness to obey so the seed can germinate in the soft and yielding soil of our souls.

God can then use his Word to probe and delve into our pride, avarice, greed, hateful thoughts, resentful grudges and indifference to human need. He can disinter the buried secrets and dark thoughts in us that so deeply defile us. He can speak to every harmful habit, every bad attitude, every troubling perspective, every destructive way of relating to others. He can begin to deal with all evil, malignant attitudes and actions—*if* we are willing to relinquish them. If we put ourselves in God's hands, he can and will begin to change us.

That's what James means by the "Perfect Law." It is perfect in that there is no law that is any better; it is *perfecting* in that there is no law that can make us any better. It is intended to move us toward God's perfect end—conformity to the character of his son, Jesus Christ.

Furthermore, the Word "gives freedom." "The wise man alone is free," said the Stoic philosophers, "and every foolish man is a slave." Freedom is not the power to do what we *want*. (That's the worst sort of slavery.) It is the power to do what we *should*—to be godlike in all we do and say.

There is power in the Word. Those who look intently into Christ's perfect law and are ready to do it, "will be blessed in their doing"— enriched and strengthened by God's grace to conform to his will. Change requires an alteration of our wills, but an alteration that cannot take place apart from Almighty intervention. Without God working through his Word we can do nothing; but with him all things are possible. "Blessed are those who hunger and thirst for righteousness," Jesus said, "for they *will* be satisfied" (Matthew 5:6).

What I'm saying is this: the greatest enjoyment of the fruitfulness of the Word is available to those who interfere with it least. The Word will do its work if we receive it with an "honest and good heart" (Luke 8:15). Those willing to cooperate with God—who will let him do whatever he wants to do, however and whenever he wants to do it—will yield a bumper crop of righteousness. God wills us whole and happy, and it will happen, if we don't get in the way.

This sentiment is one piece with what James has been saying all along: God's intention is to make us full and complete. It's not that judgment will fall on us if we fail to make the proper response to his Word, it's rather that we miss out on all the good God has in store for us.

For a plant, the failure to bear fruit is not a punishment visited upon it, but an unhappy departure from the purpose for which it was created. So with us. Resistance to God's Word means that we miss out on the very purpose for which we were made—our freedom, our fruitfulness, our fullness.

In other words, if I make a deficient response to the Word of God I have not merely failed to live up to a set of rules God made up and handed down. I have failed to live up to my identity and destiny as a man. That is my tragedy.

7

LITTLE THINGS MEAN A LOT

This quest may be attempted by the weak with as much hope as the strong. And neither strength nor wisdom will carry us far upon it. Yet such is oft the course of deeds that move the wheels of the world: small hands do them because they must, while the eyes of the great are elsewhere."

—J.R.R. Tolkien

IF ANYONE CONSIDERS HIMSELF RELIGIOUS AND YET DOES NOT KEEP A tight rein on his tongue, he deceives himself and his religion is worthless. Religion that God our Father accepts as pure and faultless is this: to look after orphans and widows in their distress and to keep oneself from being polluted by the world (James 1:26-27).

The beautiful, the special, the extraordinary are found in the ordinary if they are to be found at all, and everywhere, over everything done for Jesus' sake, no matter how small, there hovers a sense of holiness.

Holiness has to do with the small stuff of life—doing good things in secret and in silence. This is *pure* religion, James says, "to look after orphans and widows in their distress and to keep oneself from being polluted by the world."

Quiet, unpretentious deeds, done out of the way and in quietness, attack our pride, our hunger for power and prestige, our desire for recognition and approval, our determination to be important. They train us in the practice of humility, which is the essential practice of godliness.

Great acts of virtue, it seems to me, come rarely, and rarely are they hard to do. They have their own reward: the rush and recognition we get from tackling difficult and demanding endeavors, the following we attract by doing them. It's much harder to give ourselves to hidden, unheralded acts that no one sees. But these are the greatest deeds of all, the elements of which are found in no other religion, or ethical system.

Interesting word, "religion." James uses a word that seldom occurs in the New Testament. It refers to the trappings of worship: liturgy, ceremony and ritual. It is what we think of these days as the *worship* portion of a church service. "To James real worship did not lie in elaborate vestments, or in noble liturgy or in magnificent music, or in a carefully wrought service: it lay in the practical service of mankind and the purity of one's personal life" (William Barclay). Real worship shows itself in acts of charity and purity.

Some religion is "worthless," to use James' precise word, in that it has no effect on us at all. It leaves us unchanged. The one who practices that religion "deceives himself" (a phrase that takes us back to verse 22: "Do not merely listen to the word, and so *deceive*[1] yourselves"). We think we're doing well, but we're not.

This is a religion that comes of prating on about the Word, but not doing it. The Word tries to act upon us, but we will not humbly receive it and so it makes no imprint upon our souls. That religion, says James, is illusory and fanciful because it leaves us unchanged.

Pure religion shows itself in quiet, spontaneous acts of love—looking after "orphans and widows in their distress," caring for the hapless and helpless, the mournful, the friendless, the forsaken, the raga-muffins, "the wretched of the earth." It does what most people are unwilling to do. It "exaggerates what the world neglects," says G. K. Chesterton).

God is on the side of the widow and orphan, perhaps because most people in are not: "Leave your orphans (with me)," he says, "I will protect their lives. Your widows too can trust in me" (Jeremiah 49:11). He is "a father to the fatherless, a defender of widows..." (Psalm 68:5). We are most like God when we care for those he cares for.

It's interesting: nine or more times it's said that Jesus was "moved with compassion." In each case he *did* something. He healed, fed, prayed, or taught in response. He did something that assuaged suffering in some way.

The Good Samaritan was deemed "good" because he did something. The priest and Levite, who knew all the right words, did nothing. "Which of these three do you think was a neighbour to the man who fell into the hands of robbers?" Jesus asked. The lawyer replied, "The one who had compassion on him." "Go and do likewise," Jesus said (Luke 10:36,37).

Perhaps, for some, all we can do is have compassion—"feel with them," as the etymology of the word "compassion" suggests. We cannot fix them, or deal with past issues that broke them, but we can stand with them. Perhaps we can only do small things for them, but, as Mother Teresa reminded us, we can do them with great love.

It occurs to me that one way to test the authenticity of our religion is to ask ourselves to whom we gravitate as we make our way through life: to the power brokers, the shakers and movers, the beautiful people who make us feel so much better about ourselves? Or do we move toward those who have nothing going for them in this world, and who can do nothing for us? Are we willing to befriend and listen to those awkward people others avoid? Can we love them when that love seems useless; when we cannot help them? Can we care about them though they never return our affection? Can we do this in faithful obedience to God, even though no one sees or knows but he?

We can when we remember that God is the Father of all the down-trodden and disenfranchised and that includes us. We too have nothing but our wretchedness to bring to God. Only when we remember his pity for us can we speak or act in pity. Then we have a religion that God can accept.

Further, James writes, pure religion is characterized by a determination to "keep oneself from being polluted by the world." Thus he introduces that most misunderstood and misapplied concept, "the world."

The Bible says, "Love not the world," and who of us can argue with that directive. All good Christian people know that they shouldn't be like the world. But what does it mean to be worldly?

When I was growing up, worldliness was smoking, drinking, card-playing, gambling, movie-going and other scruples. But those proscriptions don't go deep enough: they don't touch the heart. It's possible for me to do, or not do any or all of them and still be polluted.

I can avoid suds and slow dancing and yet harbor rank bitterness and resentment in my soul. I can kick the smoking habit, and yet remain selfishly ambitious. I can go to prayer meetings and Bible studies, and yet gossip and spread rumors that blight and ruin the lives of my neighbors. I can avoid the cinema and all it's impurity, and yet play XXX rated scenarios in my mind and corrupt myself from the inside out. I can stay away from pool halls and poker games, and yet get bent out of shape when I'm not pampered and pandered to.

It doesn't add up and it shouldn't. It shouldn't because these conventions miss the point. The center of worldliness lies elsewhere—in the cold springs of motives and intentions, in the world's *attitudes* that pollute our souls.

Worldliness is being resentful when we're snubbed or patronized. It is smarting when our contributions are overlooked. It is reacting angrily and defensively to words spoken against us. It is growing bitter when another is preferred before us. It is harboring grudges, nursing grievances, wallowing in self–pity. These are the ways in which we're most polluted by the world.

God has something better for us: "He would have us rid of all grudging, all bitterness in word or thought, all gauging and measuring of ourselves with a different standard from that which we apply to another. He would have no curling of the lip; no indifference to the man whose service we use; no desire to excel another, no contentment at gaining by another's loss. He would not have us receive the smallest service with ingratitude; would not hear from us a tone to jar the heart of another, a word to make it ache, be the ache ever so transient" (George MacDonald). May God fill every nook and cranny of our being with that religion.

But, you say. I'll never have it in me. I'm flawed from my beginnings, cursed by some ancestor, handicapped by my parents' wrong–doing, saddled with insecurities, and sinful predilections. I can't become this sort of person.

Some of us *are* difficult cases. Flawed by environment and heredity, our personalities resist change. Yet it does no good to give up. We will only get worse if we do.

No, the only cure is to give our souls to God for his healing. He can then begin to bring about a cure. He discerns the possibilities in the

most difficult and damaged life and he can take all that's unworthy
in us and gradually turn it into good.

The process is neither swift nor painless. It often seems chaotic and
subject to agonizing delay. Progress is made not by quantum leaps
and bounds, but by a few tentative steps and a number of hard falls.
It's a creeping thing, better seen in retrospect than in prospect. Yet
every day God is taking us down the path toward the place he wants
us to be. That is our assurance.

Here's another. If you go this way you'll probably not be named or
noticed in this world, but your Father, who sees what you've done in
secret, will reward you. You will know sweet fellowship with the
One who lived to do those lowly things that others scorned and
would not do, and someday soon he will sing your praise before the
universe. "There is nothing hidden that will not be disclosed, and
nothing concealed that will not be known or brought out into the
open" (Luke 8:17).

"Only a small part is played in great deeds by any hero."

—Gandalf the Grey

8

FRIENDS IN LOW PLACES

"Christ himself was poor... and as he was himself,
so he informed his disciples, we are *all* poor...."

—Robert Burton

MY BROTHERS, AS BELIEVERS IN OUR GLORIOUS LORD JESUS CHRIST, don't show favoritism. Suppose a man comes into your meeting wearing a gold ring and fine clothes, and a poor man in shabby clothes also comes in. If you show special attention to the man wearing fine clothes and say, "Here's a good seat for you," but say to the poor man, "You stand there" or "Sit on the floor by my feet," have you not discriminated among yourselves and become judges with evil thoughts? Listen, my dear brothers: Has not God chosen those who are poor in the eyes of the world to be rich in faith and to inherit the kingdom he promised those who love him? But you have insulted the poor. Is it not the rich who are exploiting you? Are they not the ones who are dragging you into court? Are they not the ones who are slandering the noble name of him to whom you belong? If you really keep the royal law found in Scripture, "Love your neighbor as yourself," you are doing right. But if you show favoritism, you sin and are convicted by the law as law-breakers. For whoever keeps the whole law and yet stumbles at just one point is guilty of breaking all of it. For he who said, "Do not commit adultery," also said, "Do not murder." If you do not commit adultery but do commit murder, you have become a law-breaker. Speak and act as those who are going to be judged by the law that gives freedom, because judgment without mercy will be shown to anyone who has not been merciful. Mercy triumphs over judgment! (James 2:1-13).

Two men walk into a gathering: one sporting a well–tailored, expensive blue blazer, Ermenegildo Zegna tie, and tasseled Gucci loafers, polished to a high sheen; the other draped in a shabby, mustard–yellow polyester leisure suit. The first, we move over and make room for; the other we leave standing by the door. "You can't have faith in our glorious Lord Jesus Christ and show that sort of partiality, can you?" James asks.[1] Or, put another way, you can't really call yourself a Christian and be a snob.

The word James uses, translated "favoritism," here, means "to lift up the face." It has to do with a haughty countenance and a tendency to look down on other folks, as wealthy dowagers of another age peered down on lesser mortals through *lorgnettes*, a device my mother used to call, "a sneer on a stick."

To favor or disfavor anyone on the basis of birth, breeding, wealth, status, and style is to "judge with evil *thoughts*," says James. It is wrong–headed thinking—believing that the wealthy are more worthy of honor merely because they're rich, or thinking that the poor are less worthy merely because they're poor.

The old aphorism, "As a man thinks in his heart so is he," comes into play here. As a tree springs from a buried seed, so every action springs from a hidden thought. What we think is what we are; our character is formed by our thoughts.

"If a man's mind…
Hath evil thoughts, pain comes on him as comes
The wheel the ox behind…. If one endure
In purity of thought, joy follows him
As his own shadow–sure."

—James Allen

James would agree: when our thoughts are right, righteousness and joy prevail; when our thoughts are wrong, prejudice and pain are strong. "Let us endeavor to think well," said Pascal, "That is the basic principle of morality."

Here's James' first thought: "Has not God chosen those who are poor in the eyes of the world to be rich in faith and to inherit the kingdom he promised those who love him?"

It's not that God had to settle for the poor, he chose them—chose them for *himself* as the verb implies, chose them to inherit the kingdom, to enrich them beyond all measure. He is making them "Saints; gods, things like himself," C. S. Lewis said. If we could see them now as they will someday be (when God is finished with them) we would, as Lewis went on to say, fall on our knees in worship.

One early Church Father wrote, "When our little Father went about on earth, He despised no one, but sought unto the simple folk most of all. He was always among the poor folk. Those disciples of His too, He chose most of them from amongst our brother laborers like unto us—simple folk to make them great."

How can I refuse to accept and associate with one whom God has received? How can I exclude from my home and table, my friendship and love one whom God has called into fellowship with him. How can I dismiss lightly one whom God is making into a glorious god–like being? To do so is to be very much unlike our Lord, who *never* showed partiality.

Here's another thought: "Is it not the rich who are exploiting you?" James asks. Wealthy people in James' day ground the faces of the poor. These were the same who ridiculed and scorned the "fair name," the name of Jesus by which early Christians were called. Therefore, to prefer the rich and discriminate against the poor is to align oneself with the world and to become worldly in the worst sort of way.

The Old Testament suggests that in an ideal community there would be no poverty, for godly people would take care of the poor. "There should be no poor among you..." Moses assured Israel, "if only you fully obey the LORD your God and are careful to follow all these commands I am giving you today" (Deuteronomy 15:4,5).

Jesus' lament, "The poor you will always have with you," thus serves as a commentary on our cold, calculating world. Poverty continues because our culture does not care. When we pander to the rich and prosperous and overlook the poor and needy we have joined ourselves to that indifferent, unloving world around us. Once again, worldliness is not necessarily the "filthy five" of my youth (smoking, drinking, movies, dancing, card–playing). It is indifference, preference, discrimination, snobbery, prejudice and pride.

Here's James' final thought: "If you really keep the royal law found in Scripture, 'Love your neighbor as yourself,' you are doing right. But if you show favoritism, you sin and are convicted by the law as law-breakers."

James' argument is not easy to follow, but he seems to be saying that if I love a wealthy man *as a pure act of love* (without regard to his wealth), I am "doing right." If, however, I love a rich man *because* he is rich, I am "convicted as a law breaker," and am no better than an adulterer or a murderer (vs. 11).

To put it more simply, I may think of myself as a law–abiding citizen because I would never take a life, or step out on my wife, but, to put a fine point on the principle, if I'm prejudiced by age, sex, status, station, ethnic, or educational background my faith–talk, no matter how orthodox, is just so much blarney. I'm a fraud.

Prejudice, whether elitism, sexism, ageism or racism, is not a minor fault, or mere peccadillo; it is serious sin (vs. 9). To justify and defend it, rather than repent of it, suggests that I may not be a Christian at all. James minces no words: prejudice is incommensurate with true faith. I can't be a bigot and call myself a believer.

"So," James urges us, "speak (habitually) and act (habitually), as those who are to be judged by the law of liberty. For judgment will be merciless to one who has shown no mercy; mercy triumphs over judgment."

James calls us to speak and act in mercy because we will be judged by that standard. If we show mercy we will receive it; if we show no mercy none will be shown. Jesus said the same thing: "Blessed are the merciful, for they will be shown mercy" (Matthew 5:7).

These are stern words, but love must be stern at times to be kind. Father Zossima, a character in Dostoyevsky's, The Brothers Karamazov, comments, "Love in action is a harsh and dreadful thing, compared with love in dreams." Real love wants the best for the beloved even if it means damning to hell the sin that is destroying it. This is James' love.

Let's get one thing straight: James is not suggesting that mercy has purchasing power. Showing mercy to others does not obligate God to show mercy to us. Our mercy is only *evidential* in that it demonstrates that we understand the depth of our misery and the incredible mercy of God in accepting us in that state.

Jesus made the same point in his parable about the steward who was forgiven a debt he could never repay ($10,000,000 in today's dollars), and who therefore, was expected by his master to extend mercy to a debtor who owed him a very small sum ($1.80). That he failed to do so was an indication that he did not understand the enormity of his own debt and the unthinkable grace his Master had shown in forgiving it (*cf.* Matthew 18:21–35). Therefore, he was, in fact, an unforgiven man.

God has given mercy and that giving teaches us to render mercy to all. The proof and sure evidence that we have received God's mercy and the gift of eternal life is the simple sharing of all the good we have received. Mercy is not the means by which we receive mercy, but the mark of one who has already received it, and whose heart has been enlarged by God's love. There is no prejudice in that person and thus there is no condemnation.

How do I know I have received grace? Because I am gracious. How do I know I have received mercy? Because I am merciful. Thus, "mercy triumphs over judgment," or, to preserve the meaning of James' verb: "mercy *shouts out loud!*" My salvation comes through loud and clear.

Thus James completes the circle and brings us back to his premise: You can't call yourself a Christian and be a snob. Real Christians are known by their love.

9

FAITH THAT WORKS

"One who learns in order to teach
will be enabled to learn and to teach;
but one who learns in order to practice
will be enabled to learn and to teach,
to preserve and to practice."

—Yishma'el, son of Rabbi Yochanan ben Beroka, *Mishnah of
Pirkei Avot*

WHAT GOOD IS IT, MY BROTHERS, IF A MAN CLAIMS TO HAVE FAITH BUT
has no deeds? Can such faith save him? Suppose a brother or sister is
without clothes and daily food. If one of you says to him, "Go, I wish
you well; keep warm and well fed," but does nothing about his
physical needs, what good is it? In the same way, faith by itself, if it
is not accompanied by action, is dead. But someone will say, "You
have faith; I have deeds." Show me your faith without deeds, and I
will show you my faith by what I do. You believe that there is one
God. Good! Even the demons believe that—and shudder. You foolish
man, do you want evidence that faith without deeds is useless? Was

not our ancestor Abraham considered righteous for what he did when he offered his son Isaac on the altar? You see that his faith and his actions were working together, and his faith was made complete by what he did. And the scripture was fulfilled that says, "Abraham believed God, and it was credited to him as righteousness," and he was called God's friend. You see that a person is justified by what he does and not by faith alone. In the same way, was not even Rahab the prostitute considered righteous for what she did when she gave lodging to the spies and sent them off in a different direction? As the body without the spirit is dead, so faith without deeds is dead (James 2:14-26).

Snoopy crouches in blowing snow at Charlie Brown's door with his food dish clamped between his teeth. "Go! Be warmed and filled!" chimes Charlie Brown—and shuts the door. "What good is that?" Snoopy mutters as he trudges back to his doghouse. James' point exactly.

"What good is it if a man claims to have faith, but has no deeds? Can *that* faith save him?"[1] No, indeed. Faith cannot exist apart from holiness.

Real faith regenerates. If it is not changing me into another, better version of myself my faith is at best defective, or worse, it may be stone, cold dead. This is the inescapable conclusion to which James keeps drawing us in his book.

Martin Luther, as I pointed out in the introduction, was at first troubled by James' emphasis on deeds, which is why he saddled the work with that dubious epithet, "an epistle of straw." His initial antipathy was based on his perception that James and Paul were at variance. James, he thought, flatly contradicted Paul's emphasis that we are saved not by works but by faith and faith *alone* (Romans 3:28). For that reason, Luther thought James was a seriously defective and dangerous book, but he was wrong, as he later admitted.

While Paul does state clearly that faith alone saves us, he is in agreement with James that *saving* faith will always manifest itself in loving deeds. The two are inextricably linked.[2] "The *only* thing that counts," he wrote on one occasion, "is faith expressing itself through love" (Galatians 5:6).

What James is protesting is not Pauline theology, but a perversion of it: acting as though God's Word is mere advice and wending our own way. Few Christians would ever put it quite so baldly, but in effect that's the way many so-called believers live. They say, "We believe," but there's nothing to distinguish them from unbelievers. They live by their own lusts rather than by the will of God.

How sad that we would claim to be Jesus' follower and go our own way. (I recall Ambrose Bierce's bitter definition of Christians as those "who believe in the teachings of Jesus Christ insofar as they are not inconsistent with a life of sin.") It only confirms the world in its opinion that we Christians are up to no good and makes unbelievers by the score. How sad—indeed, how tragic. Can that "faith" save us? Can it draw others to salvation? "No, indeed!" says James.

James then introduces an imaginary associate who argues his case (a common rhetorical device in those days): "You have faith; I have deeds. Show me your faith without deeds, and I will show you my faith by what I do."

We are not saved by works, nor could we ever be, but our works *show* that we are thoroughly saved. If others cannot see God's love in us we do not have *saving* faith and thus we are not Christians at all, no matter what we say. "Faith without works is *dead*."

Furthermore, faith without works is *demonic*: "You believe there is one God?" he asks, "Good for you! Even the demons believe that truth, and their hair stands on end!"[3]

Demons are fully informed believers—better informed than we are because they're closer to the source. There are no heretics among the demons in hell; they "do good theology" there. But they don't love

God, nor do they love one another. They *believe,* but their beliefs do not touch their hearts, nor do they transform their character. Demons are demonic to the end.

Faith, you see, is more than informed belief—more than knowing *what* to do. It is a profoundly intimate relationship with God that involves agreement of mind, body and soul with all that God has in mind for us and *doing* it no matter what our circumstances are, or how we feel about it. Anything else is just words.

As examples of authentic faith James adduces two true believers: Abraham and Rahab.

Abraham, James tells us, was "considered righteous for what he *did*..." He was asked to put his only son to death, the son through which God had promised to save the world. It made no sense to obey, yet he did so, trusting that God could raise Isaac from the dead if necessary (Hebrews 11:19). Abraham's faith and actions "worked together" as James puts it, and demonstrated the integrity of his faith. He *did* what God asked him to do and thus showed us he had the real thing.

And then there was Rahab, the Canaanite temple prostitute (cited here, perhaps, as a reminder of the old idea that sins of passion may lead us to God while sins of pride will not). Rahab heard of Israel's God and longed for him until his messengers came to bring salvation to her. She then put her faith on the line, trusting God in that dangerous moment when she shielded the spies and saw them safely on their way. Rahab's faith, though primitive, was pure and issued in immediate efforts to further the purposes of the God of Israel. "Was not Rahab the prostitute considered righteous for what she *did* when she gave lodging to the spies and sent them off in a different direction?" James asks. Rahab had the only faith worth having.

So, James concludes, faith is more than agreement with historic creed and the good intentions that are aroused by that creed. It is deeds— faith expressing itself in love.

Few things are more dangerous than intellectual assent that does not touch the heart, or good intentions that die on the vine. Every time we do not obey, or mean to obey and do not, we harden our hearts a little and make it less likely that we will ever obey. "Good notions must take advantage of their first ripeness," George MacDonald said. "We mustn't try the Spirit with our delays."

Authentic faith does not agree with truth and think someday we will do it. It takes God at his word and does what he says as soon as possible. He does not ask us to do everything at once, nor does he ask us to do things that are impossible to do, but he does ask (and sometimes he asks hard things), and when he asks we must be willing to obey. This is saving faith.

But, you say, I can't keep the faith. Not to worry. God knows you better than you know yourself, and he has a way. "Faith comes from hearing, and hearing by the word of Christ" (Romans 10:17). Authentic faith—faith that bears much fruit—is the product of the Word.

An older generation of spiritual mentors referred to the practice of "spiritual reading," which is more than mere Bible study. It is reading with a desire to be thoroughly transformed by God's Word. It is "reading with a heart ready to repent" (Sister Macrina Wiederkehr).

It's easy for us to get caught up in curiosity and speculation and the pride that comes from acquiring facts about God, but approaching the Word that way only takes us farther away from our Lord. Truth never gets out of our minds and into our hearts. "We become talking heads," Carolyn says, "biblical pundits, who are sources, scholars and critics, but who have no heart for God." Bible study that stops short of response becomes a tool of the devil to make us like the other denizens of hell—full of truth and ungodliness.

No, spiritual reading is something more. It is reading God's word until our hearts are touched. There's no need to read any number of verses, nor is there any rush to get through. When our hearts are touched, we can stop reading.

A touched heart means that God's word has come. He has entered in and is speaking to us. Then we can begin to think about what he is saying to us.

Jeremiah said, "When your words *came*, I ate them...."(Jeremiah 15:16). We must sink our teeth into the word and chew it with our minds and hearts. We must come to grips with it, wrestle with it, struggle with it, ask questions of it, allow it to sink in.

We must ask ourselves what this word means to us, what are its implications, what must we do or undo. Then we must pray that God will make us true to the truth, for without him we can do nothing. There is an ancient Dominican prayer that well sums up that intention:

> *Why has my heart been touched?*
> *How am I to be changed through this touch?*
> *I need to change; I need to look a little more like You.*
> *May these sacred words change and transform me.*

Another early Christian states the same thought this way: "Read under the eye of God until your heart is touched, then give yourself up to love" (Dom Guigo).

It's safe to give ourselves up to God's love. He created us out of love and his love is never wearied or worn out by our sins. He is relentless in his pursuit of us and in his determination that one day we will be pure love, at whatever cost to us, or to himself.

"Good and upright is the LORD," the psalmist reminds us, and "*therefore* he instructs sinners in his ways. He guides the humble in what is right and teaches them his way" (Psalm 25:8,9). The only requirement is humility and the patience to wait for his working. God is not known for haste, but he does mean business.

THAT WORKS | 53

Thy doors are deeds; the handles are their doing.
He whose day–life is obedient righteousness,
Who, after failure, or a poor success,
Rises up, stronger effort yet renewing,
He finds thee, Lord, at length, in his own common room.

—*The Diary of an Old Soul*

"But I don't know how to rise up," you say. Here's what you must do.

Prepare yourself to do something the Lord has asked you to do. Instead of asking yourself whether you believe it or not, ask yourself whether you've done one thing today simply because Jesus said, "Do it," or abstained because he said, "Don't do it." We can't say we believe or even want to believe, if we aren't willing do anything he tells us.

"You can begin at once to be a disciple of the Living One," George MacDonald said, "by obeying him in the first thing you can think of in which you are not obeying him. We must learn to obey him in everything, and so must begin somewhere. Let it be at once, and in the very next thing that lies at the door of our conscience."

I search my heart —I search, and find no faith...
No good seems likely. To and fro I am hurled.
I have to stay. Only obedience holds —
I haste, I rise, I do the thing he saith.

10

THE TELLTALE TONGUE

Earth's wisest sages this impart:
The tongue's great storehouse is the heart.

—Folk proverb

NOT MANY OF YOU SHOULD PRESUME TO BE TEACHERS, MY BROTHERS, because you know that we who teach will be judged more strictly. We all stumble in many ways. If anyone is never at fault in what he says, he is a perfect man, able to keep his whole body in check. When we put bits into the mouths of horses to make them obey us, we can turn the whole animal. Or take ships as an example. Although they are so large and are driven by strong winds, they are steered by a very small rudder wherever the pilot wants to go. Likewise the tongue is a small part of the body, but it makes great boasts. Consider what a great forest is set on fire by a small spark. The tongue also is a fire, a world of evil among the parts of the body. It corrupts the whole person, sets the whole course of his life on fire, and is itself set on fire by hell. All kinds of animals, birds, reptiles and creatures of the sea are being tamed and have been tamed by man, but no man can tame the tongue. It is a restless evil, full of deadly poison. With the tongue we praise our Lord and Father, and with it we curse men, who have been made in God's likeness. Out of the same mouth come praise and cursing. My brothers, this should not be. Can both fresh water and salt water flow from the same spring? My brothers, can a fig-tree bear olives, or a grapevine bear figs? Neither can a salt spring produce fresh water (James 3:1-12).

Nothing is easier than sinning and there are many ways to sin, but mostly we sin by what we say. "How much must I be changed before I am changed," as old John Donne would say.

Actually, James goes beyond our words and looks deep down into our hearts. Not only do we sin by what we say, he insists, but what we say is the measure of our sinfulness: "If anyone is never at fault in what he says, he is a perfect man, able to keep his whole body in check." "Stick out your tongue," says Dr. James. "I want to see the state of your soul." Thus James begins his treatise on the tongue.

The tongue is a little member, he observes, yet it can do great things. Three metaphors make his point: little bits control strong horses; little rudders turn mighty sailing ships; little sparks ignite vast conflagrations. Little things mean a lot.

The tongue, though very small, "makes great boasts." "Look what I can do," it struts and brags. "I can ruin a reputation. I can destroy a life work. I can rupture a long–standing relationship. I can crush the strongest spirit. I can spoil the tenderest moment. I can humiliate, embarrass and shame. I can curse and cut and kill!"

"(The tongue) is the world of evil among the parts of the body," adds James —not *a* world, but *the* world, a microcosm, a little world within us. All that is in the world, the lust of the flesh, the lust of the eyes, the pride of life, the tongue suggests, commits and condones. Anything the world can do the tongue can do it and do it better.

Here again is the world—the world of attitudes—gossip, deceit, exaggeration, discourtesy, impurity, harshness, impatience and every other transgression.

"(The tongue)," says James, "corrupts the whole person, sets the whole course of his life on fire, and is itself set on fire by hell." The tongue defiles every part of our being and every moment of our lives, from the cradle to the grave. It burns its way through our "life cycle" to use James' exact expression, like an out-of-control forest fire, leaving devastation and ruin. Only in our death will it die. In the words of an old tombstone inscription,

> BENEATH THIS STONE, A LUMP OF CLAY
> LIES ROBERT ANDREW YOUNG,
> WHO, ON THE TWENTY–FOURTH OF MAY,
> BEGAN TO HOLD HIS TONGUE.

That could be my epitaph as well.

James' phrase "(the tongue) is set on fire by hell," is evocative. His word for hell is *gehenna*, Jerusalem's garbage dump, a fitting metaphor for hell in those days, associated as it was with impurity, corruption, fumes and stench, a place ruled by Baalzebub, the Lord of the Flies[1]—the source of the filth that so readily rolls off our tongues.

And here's the worst of it: "no man can tame the tongue." Every other living thing has been domesticated, or dominated by the human race, but the human tongue cannot be captured, caged or killed. "You can tame a tiger," *The Message* says, "but you can not tame a tongue—it's never been done." It is a restless, vicious, venomous, feral thing that *cannot* be controlled—at least it cannot be controlled by "man."

Finally, James notes an odd incongruity: with our tongues we bless God and curse men, the most god–like beings on earth. Blessings and curses from the same orifice. "My brethren," says James in a masterpiece of understatement, "these things ought not to be this way."

Who can explain this strange ambivalence? James' answer is to consider the source:

> Does a fountain send out from the same opening
> both fresh and bitter water?
> Can a fig tree, my brethren, produce olives,
> or a vine produce figs?
> Neither can salt water produce fresh.

Fresh water flows from fresh subterranean sources; bitter water from deep springs of bitterness. James doesn't explain his metaphor. He lets it hang in the air and leaves it for us to think it out. That's the best thing you can do for another, George MacDonald said: "Wake things up that are in him; or make him think out things for himself."

Having thought about it for a while, here's what I believe James has in mind. Our words are formed deep within in our hearts. Good words come from the good in us; evil words flow from the evil we have accumulated within. If we want to deal with our tongues we've got to get our minds right.

Jesus put it in clear and concise language: "No good tree bears bad fruit, nor does a bad tree bear good fruit. Each tree is recognized by its own fruit. People do not pick figs from thorn–bushes, or grapes from briers. The good man brings good things out of the good stored up in his heart, and the evil man brings evil things out of the evil stored up in his heart. For out of the overflow of his heart his mouth speaks" (Luke 6:43–45).

The heart is the storehouse of the body. We must careful, then, of the things we put inside it. They can become words at any moment.

How can we get our words right? We must fill our thoughts with God's words—*meditate* on them day and night. The secret of good words is the Word of God, delighted in and meditated upon, for what is the Word of God, but the life of God which always translates itself into human speech.

Let me illustrate how this works for me, at least in one situation (though I must say I don't always make it work). Certain folks "bring out the worst in me" (interesting phrase). I find it unnatural and, in some cases, impossible to curb my tongue when I'm around them. Like David, my heart grows hot within me, and as I *meditate* (here's that word again) the fire burns and I speak with my tongue (Psalm 39:3). At best I'm curt and discourteous; at worst I give them a "piece of my *mind*."

"Aha! I say." The problem is not my words, you see, but my *mind*. Long before I open my mouth I have opened my mind to wrong–thinking. I have rehearsed the wrong done to me by my brother. I have nursed my hurt feelings. I have imputed wrong motives. I have pandered to self pity and pride. I have harbored resentment and rage. "The fire burns and I speak with my tongue." My heated words have been created and shaped by my thoughts long before they spill out of my mouth. How can anything clean come from something unclean?

Paul says, "Whatever is true, whatever is noble, whatever is right, whatever is pure, whatever is lovely, whatever is admirable—if anything is excellent or praiseworthy—*think about such things*" (Philippians 4:8). He's not suggesting that I give myself to noble abstractions, as good as that may be, but rather that I focus on those attributes in *others* that are true, noble, righteous, pure, admirable and loveable.

In other words, instead of obsessing over the wrong that I see in others, I must focus on the good God is doing in them. (It's not just Christians who have good things going for them. Every human being is a recipient of God's common grace.) When I do so, their "small asperities of spirit disappear, lost in the grander curves of character" (Ambrose Bierce). I see blessedness where before I saw only sin. I see loveliness and beauty that eludes me until I look at them in the light of the love of Jesus. My heart begins to soften and my words are more inclined to follow in kind.

There is this, however: I never find it easy to think God's thoughts after him, especially under duress. All hell conspires to make me forget what I know. "It is funny how mortals always picture us as putting things into their minds," Screwtape wrote to his demonic nephew. "In reality our best work is done in keeping things out."

We must, therefore, meditate on God's thoughts day and night to keep them on our minds. And we must pray as David Elginbrod prayed, "Grant that more an' more thoughts o' Thy thinking may come into our hearts day by day."

GENTLE WISDOM

Where wisdom is, there happiness will crown
A piety that nothing will corrode.
But high and mighty words and ways
Are flogged to humbleness, till age,
Beaten to its knees, at last is wise.

—Sophocles

WHO IS WISE AND UNDERSTANDING AMONG YOU? LET HIM SHOW IT BY his good life, by deeds done in the humility that comes from wisdom. But if you harbor bitter envy and selfish ambition in your hearts, do not boast about it or deny the truth. Such "wisdom" does not come down from heaven but is earthly, unspiritual, of the devil. For where you have envy and selfish ambition, there you find disorder and every evil practice. But the wisdom that comes from heaven is first of all pure; then peace–loving, considerate, submissive, full of mercy and good fruit, impartial and sincere. Peacemakers who sow in peace raise a harvest of righteousness (James 3:13-18).

. . .

Wisdom in the Bible originally meant technical expertise, or the ability to do a job well. It was skillfulness in dealing with whatever was at hand. And, since the matter at hand was always life itself, wisdom came to mean "skill at life," or "the capacity to live life as it *ought* to be lived." The wise are those who live well, and who, when finished, have something to show for it. They have accomplished something eternally worthwhile.

However, (here's the important thing) it's not what we *know* that makes us wise, but what we *are*. James makes that very clear: "Let the wise man show his wisdom by his *good life*, by deeds done in the humility that comes from wisdom." Wisdom is the "good life," or, more precisely, the "beautiful life"—a holy, genial presence that makes visible the life of our invisible Lord.

Wisdom is the essence of the spiritual life and the means by which everything is done. It is the dynamic that draws others to God, if they are to be drawn at all. It is the most powerful force on earth. Remember Peter's words: "Live good (beautiful) lives among the pagans so that…they may see your good deeds and glorify God on the day he visits us" (1 Peter 2:12). This is wisdom.

It's far better to be wise than well–informed because, as James warns us, knowledge alone is counter–productive. It gets past our hearts and goes to our heads. It riddles our thoughts with "bitter envy and selfish ambition," and where these motivations and agendas exist, James assures us, "there is disorder and every evil practice." Without wisdom, no matter how well–informed and well–intentioned we may be, we will soon find ourselves doing the work of the devil.

What then is this "wisdom from heaven" of which James speaks?

- It is *pure*—morally pure, yet not puritanical in the pejorative sense of the word. It is not a strictness, severity and distaste for joy and pleasure, but love for all that is good and true and beautiful. We are pure when we take joy in what is pure; impure when we take joy in impurity. The things we love and take delight in tell us what we are.

- It is *peaceful*—tranquil, restful and composed. Peace is the action of those who are aligned heart to heart with God and who are quiet and confident in his will (Psalm 131:2). Wisdom is calm and relaxed; it is rarely in a hurry. It is not enraptured and enslaved by the rush and frenzy of this world, but has about it the leisurely perspective of eternity. It can wait while God goes about his business and gets things done in his time and in his way.

- It is *considerate*, a word used in the ancient world for fine, old wine. Wisdom is not harsh or acerbic, but fragrant and agreeable. It is mellow—easy to work with and live with, fun to be with, gentle on the mind.

- It is *submissive*, or, as the Authorized Version puts it, "easy to be entreated." It is not unrepentant, uncorrectable, hard–headed and intractable. It is teachable, reasonable, willing to listen, willing to be persuaded, willing to yield when it can and must.

- It is *full of mercy*. It empathizes with the limitations and failures of others and handles the most fragile and intensely personal things with sensitivity and compassion. It understands the heartache of a lonely, cold marriage, or a rebel child and weeps for the hardness of the world. It knows the pain of physical ailment and overwhelming debt, the scars of neglect and humiliation, the silences of God. It absorbs the weakness and failure of others—even irritability and anger—and returns love and patience as a gift.

- It is *impartial*. It does not separate, discriminate or play favorites. It regards no one from a worldly point of view, but sees the least and lowest of human beings as they could be if only they were in Christ (2 Corinthians 5:16,17). It views all people as neighbors and loves them with the impartial, unprejudiced love that caused God to give himself wholly to the world.

- It is *sincere*. It does not pose, act a part, or deliberately deceive. It does not deal in false humility, false meekness and all the other subtle hypocrisies to which we Christians are so susceptible. It is honest, unpretentious, transparent. It intends to do what it knows to do and admits to what it cannot yet do.

These qualities James describes as *"gentle* wisdom,"[1] an idea that's difficult to translate precisely, but which suggests a quality of mercy that goes beyond the demands of justice. It forgives when it has every right to condemn. It considers others' frailty in the face of their failures and offers pity in the place of judgment. It has compassion even on those who are responsible for the fixes in which they find themselves. It does not say, "You've made your bed now lie in it," but reaches out in love and compassion to help the sinner rise from his bed. It is kind, gentle and forgiving beyond human comprehension.

Jonathan Edwards wrote, "Gentleness may well be called the Christian spirit. It is the distinguishing disposition in the hearts of Christians to be identified as Christians. All who are truly godly have a gentle spirit in them."

Such wisdom cannot be gained from others, nor can it be obtained on our own. It is not a product of intellect, education, experience or long, slow, steady thinking. It "comes from above" as James puts it. It is achieved not by striving, but by hungering, praying—and waiting.

Time is an essential part of the process. We grow "slowly wise," but we *can* grow and we *will* grow as wisdom is given to us from above. And as we practice what we have been given, a deep thirst will awaken in us for more—and more will be given. "Whoever has will be given more, and he will have an abundance" (Matthew 13:12).

Most of us live fairly unremarkable lives. We're not miracle–workers, nor are we noted for anything in particular. We're not important, nor are we essential; we're just plain, ordinary, common–place folks. But those who are heavenly–wise need never worry about being ignored or irrelevant. Though often nameless, they are never useless. They sow an enduring harvest.

Paul says, "We are to God the aroma of Christ among those who are being saved and those who are perishing...(2 Corinthians 2:15,16). That's the thing about wisdom. The wise don't have to press. They don't have to fob off or foist their faith on anyone. They just leave it behind. Wherever they go and whatever they do they sow seeds of righteousness that spring up in others to eternal life. This is the lasting legacy of the wise. It is the way they make their mark on the world.

"The only way to make people good is to *be* good," mused George MacDonald, "Remember the beam and the mote."

12

WAR AND PEACE

"The sole cause of wars and revolutions and battles
is nothing other than desire."

—Plato

WHAT CAUSES FIGHTS AND QUARRELS AMONG YOU? DON'T THEY COME
from your desires that battle within you? You want something but
don't get it. You kill and covet, but you cannot have what you want.
You quarrel and fight. You do not have, because you do not ask God.
When you ask, you do not receive, because you ask with wrong
motives, that you may spend what you get on your pleasures. You
adulterous people, don't you know that friendship with the world is
hatred towards God? Anyone who chooses to be a friend of the
world becomes an enemy of God. Or do you think Scripture says
without reason that the spirit he caused to live in us envies
intensely? But he gives us more grace. That is why Scripture says:
"God opposes the proud but gives grace to the humble." Submit
yourselves, then, to God. Resist the devil, and he will flee from you.
Come near to God and he will come near to you. Wash your hands,

you sinners, and purify your hearts, you double-minded. Grieve, mourn and wail. Change your laughter to mourning and your joy to gloom. Humble yourselves before the Lord, and he will lift you up (James 4:1-10).

What causes fights and quarrels—border disputes, racial tensions, family squabbles, marital spats, sibling rivalry? Why is there so much discord and dissonance in the world? Why can't we get along? James answers his own question: controversies arise because, "You want something and don't get it."

James swings his axe at the root of the problem—a smothering absorption with ourselves—getting what we want when we want it. Frustrated in the pursuit of our own well–being we resort to rage and cruel force.

Conflict stems from "desire," says James, a Greek word from which we get our word "hedonism."[1] Hedonism is the notion that only what is pleasant or has pleasant consequences is intrinsically good. Taken to its extreme it's the relentless and ruthless pursuit of personal pleasure without regard for others.

There are no bad or unlawful pleasures. "*Everything* God created is good, and nothing is to be rejected if it is received with thanksgiving, because it is consecrated (put to its intended use) by the word of God and prayer" (1 Timothy 4: 4,5). "Pleasures are shafts of glory," C. S. Lewis states, intimations of God's goodness and love, serendipitous occasions of his grace.

Nor is there anything wrong with desiring pleasure or seeking it. Pleasures only become unlawful when they are snatched in the wrong way, or at the wrong time. It is the *stealing* of a watermelon that is wrong, not the melon.

The trouble comes when the pursuit of pleasure puts us in conflict with another human being similarly inclined. Two people desire a pleasurable thing, but both cannot have it at once. (Two drivers converging on the last parking space at a crowded mall comes to mind.) One or the other is thwarted in his desire, a frustration that can soon escalate into anger, blows and lethal rage. "You want something, but don't get it, (so) you *kill*." (It is a fact that most homicides are not premeditated acts, but "crimes of passion," as we say, prompted by frustration and deeply regretted after the fact.) The unguarded pursuit of pleasure can lead to terrifying violence. James does well to warn us.

Every evil in the world springs from unrestrained desire. "It is insatiable desires which overturn not only individual men, but whole families, and which even bring down the state. From desires there spring hatred, schisms, discords, seditions and wars," wrote Cicero, the Roman statesman.

Philo, Cicero's Jewish near–contemporary, said much the same: "Is it not because of desire that relations are broken, and natural goodwill changed into desperate enmity, that great and populous countries are desolated by domestic dissensions, and land and sea filled with ever new disasters by naval battles and land campaigns? For wars famous in tragedy…have all flowed from one source—desire for money, or glory or pleasure. Over these things the human race goes mad."[2] Undisciplined, unrestrained desire is at the root of all that is wrong with our world.

James' solution is profoundly simple: when you want something and can't get it—ask God for it. When your need for human love and approval is frustrated—ask God. When your hunger for appreciation and respect is ungratified—ask God. When your desire for peace and quiet is hindered—ask God. When in the pursuit of *any* pleasure you collide with someone pursuing his or her pleasure, rather than insist that *your* needs be met—ask God. He is the giver of every good and perfect gift and it delights his heart to give. If our needs are not met, James says, it is simply because we have not asked.

But there is one proviso: we must ask with a quiet and submitted will. We cannot dictate the time or terms of our satisfaction. It may be that God will give us what we want, but give it to us later than we would like to have it. It may be that he will not give us what we want at all. He may ask us to forgo the thing we want, but he will give us the satisfaction we are seeking. It's not the thing we seek that matters anyway—it fades and is forgotten. It's the joy that accompanies it. Authentic joy is an effect quite apart from any natural cause.

What this means is that we must give our deepest desires to God and let him satisfy us *his* way. The alternative—taking matters into our own hands—James calls adultery. It's an apt metaphor. When we seek satisfaction on our own and apart from God's love, we are unfaithful to the lover of our souls who longs to satisfy each desire of our heart.

Furthermore, James continues, such unfaithfulness is "friendship with the world." It aligns us with the world's way of doing things—its motivations, methods and moods. Here again is worldliness: the uncompromising pursuit of pleasure, making *our* good the highest good. It's nothing more than self-centeredness and pride. Of all interfering things pride is the worst for it keeps us from God and all that he has in mind for us. That's why he must oppose it and, if necessary, bring us to our knees. Only then can he do good things for us.

There is, however, an alternative to God's humbling: we can "humble ourselves." We can submit to his will—acknowledge his right to give us what we want his way. By so doing we "resist the devil," who is behind our restless, loveless self-seeking. "And with that (by drawing near) Apollyon spread forth his dragon wings, and sped him away, that Christian saw him no more" (John Bunyan, *The Pilgrim's Progress*).

We can "draw near to God" in prayer. When we do so he will draw near and meet us in that quiet place. In his presence we find the satisfaction we crave.

We must "wash our hands and purify our hearts"—cleanse ourselves from all selfish actions and attitudes that defile us and demean others. Self–derived, self–centered pleasure is not a small indiscretion, or a slight impoliteness, but a deadly perversion. We ought to "grieve, mourn and wail" over it. The least bit of selfishness is serious sin indeed.

Then, having humbled ourselves, God will exalt us, lift us higher than we were before. The thing we sought—the thing we thought we must have—is lost in the pure pleasure of God–given delight.

Bernard of Clairvaux wrote long ago, "What will you do if your needs are not met? Will you look to God to meet your needs? God promises that those who seek first the kingdom and his righteousness will have all things added to them. God promises that to those who restrict themselves and give to their neighbor he will give whatever is necessary. Seeking first the kingdom means to prefer to bear the yoke of modesty and restraint rather than allow sin to reign in your mortal body" (from *On the Love of God*).

Asking God to meet our needs is much better than getting what we want our way, for, as James puts it, God gives a "greater grace" (4:6) —greater than anything we could ever get on our own.

13

PLAYING GOD AND OTHER PERILS

Here lie I, Martin Elginbrode:
Have mercy o' my soul, Lord God,
As I would do were I Lord God,
And Ye were Martin Elginbrode.

—Epitaph in a Scottish graveyard

BROTHERS, DO NOT SLANDER ONE ANOTHER. ANYONE WHO SPEAKS against his brother or judges him speaks against the law and judges it. When you judge the law, you are not keeping it, but sitting in judgment on it. There is only one Lawgiver and Judge, the one who is able to save and destroy. But you—who are you to judge your neighbor? (James 4:11,12).

The etymology of James' word, "slander," suggests "speaking *down*." Linked with his other word, "judging," it implies an inclination to put a brother down. Paul makes a similar observation, "Why do you

judge your brother? Or why do you *look down* on your brother?"
(Romans 14:10).

Certainly it's unacceptable to tolerate wrong actions, or condone an
environment that allows wrong actions to occur. In the midst of our
culture's addled and confused notion of tolerance—a tolerance that
says we cannot critique anyone's idea of right and wrong—we must
know it's okay to know what one should and should not do. God has
given his word and calls on us to discern between good and evil;
good judgment is a mark of maturity. As G. K. Chesterton pointed
out, "Morality, like art, consists of drawing a straight line."

Some have made Jesus' words, "Judge not that you be not judged,"
an admonition to turn a blind eye to other's faults, but that can't be
what he meant when in the same breath he says that we should not
"give dogs what is sacred" or "throw pearls to pigs" (Matthew 7:6).
That caution assumes that we can and must recognize cynical and
profane people when we see them. In the same way, Jesus admon-
ished his disciples to "judge for yourselves what is right" (Luke
12:57).

Jesus' and James' injunctions against judging are not about drawing
straight lines, but about condemning others and writing them off—
judging them without mercy and without caring for their souls. Put
another way, judging, in the sense James employs the word, is a
matter of being *merely* just.

It's good that God is not merely just. If he were we would be in a
world of trouble, for he would judge every one of us at this moment.
He would put down cruel and monstrous tyrants everywhere, true,
but he would also put down our cruelty and petty tyranny. "Are not
the gods just?" C. S. Lewis' Psyche, asks her wise mentor. "Oh, no,
my child," was the reply. "Where would we be if they were?"

I recall a conversation between Robinson Crusoe and his Man
Friday: "Well," says Friday, "you say God is so strong, so great: has
he not as much strong, as much might as the devil?"

"Yes, yes, Friday," Crusoe replied, "God is much stronger than the devil."

"But if God much strong, much might as the devil, why God no kill the devil so make him no more do wicked?"

"You might as well ask," Crusoe answered reflectively, "Why does God not kill you and me when we do wicked things that offend?"

The point is that God has every right to kill you and me instantly the moment we do any wicked thing, but he has chosen to show compassion. God will judge the world in due time—"when the sun grows old, and the stars are cold, then the judgment book unfold"—but for now he is reserving final judgment. Would that you and I were more like our Father.

I know the world in which I live, a world of my own, the narrow world of my mind—haughty, unforgiving, and judgmental. How readily I pronounce judgment on others' motives and behavior though I have neither the knowledge nor the authority to do so.

Calvin wrote, "Our indulgence ought to extend to tolerating imperfections of conduct... There always have been persons who, imbued with a false persuasion of absolute holiness, as if they had already become a kind of aerial spirits, spurn the society of all in whom they see that something human still remains."

Judging others doesn't seem like much of a sin, but James would have us believe it's a serious breach of the Law of Love (James 2:8). When I condemn my brother I'm not a lover but a judge—a judge of my own brother and of my Father's law, interpreting it and modifying it to mean what I think it ought to mean—rescinding it on occasion. Better that I love my brother as he is and let God deal with his imperfections. That's "sloppy *agape*" you say. I say I'd rather love too many than too few.

Furthermore, when I condemn my brother I'm playing God—infringing on his rights as the judge of all the earth. "There is only

one Lawgiver and Judge, the one who is able to save and destroy,"
says James. Then his bony finger rises out of the text and points
directly at me: "But you (Yes, I'm talking to *you!*)—who are you to
judge your neighbor?" (James 4:12).

Some actions are easy to identify as sin, but judging is much more
elusive. It's hard to know the difference between discernment and
ungodly condemnation. Where exactly is the line? I don't always
know and even when I do I don't always get it right, but here are
some thoughts that have helped me.

There's a firm maxim that all right judgment of my brother begins
with *self*-judgment. I cannot discern another's sin until I sit in judgment on my own. "How can you say to your brother, 'Let me take
the speck out of your eye,' when all the time there is a plank in your
own eye?" (Matthew 7:4). When confronted with a brother's offenses
the humble heart turns first to itself and to God.

Further, I must not go "beyond what is written" (1 Corinthians 4:6)
and make binding for others what scripture does not bind. It's
possible for me to judge a brother not because he's unlike Jesus, but
because he's unlike *me*. I need to know that others can be strange,
off-beat, eccentric, unusual, and marching to a different drummer
without being sinful and morally out of step. "Who are you to judge
someone else's servant?" Paul says of my private scruples, "To his
own master he stands or falls. And he will stand, for the Lord is able
to make him stand" (Romans 14:4). Where scripture is silent I must
be silent.

Finally, I must not judge another's motives. I've never seen a motive,
and wouldn't know one if I saw it. I can never say, "You did this
because...." Heart-motives are beyond my ken.

Scripture is full of examples of mistaken assumptions, like those of
Job's friends who were convinced his suffering was the result of
profound sin. Yet, they were wrong. Only God saw the whole
picture. With the limited insight we have a faulty verdict is assured.

It's good to ask those who seem to have gone wrong, "Can you tell me why you did what you did?" We may be surprised at what we learn. Even if we can't fully understand another's intentions it will help us become more understanding. "The purposes of a man's heart are deep waters," reads the proverb, "but a man of understanding draws them out" (Proverbs 20:5). It's an old saying: "Know another's burden and then you won't be able to speak except in pity."

Some years ago I heard a true story that somewhat illustrates this insight. It seems there was a young salesman who worked for a company whose president gave turkeys to all his employees at Christmas. The man was a bachelor, didn't know how to roast a turkey and didn't particularly want to learn, so the gift was only a complication as far as he was concerned. Every year he had to figure out how to rid himself of the thing.

On the day the turkeys were handed out, a couple of the man's friends purloined the bird tagged with his name and substituted a dummy made of paper mache. The only original turkey–parts were the neck and tail protruding from either end of the brown paper wrapper.

The bogus bird was then presented with due formality, and our man, with turkey tucked under his arm, caught his bus for home.

As it happened, he seated himself next to a man whose melancholy was obvious. Feeling compassion for him, the salesman began a conversation in which the other man's bitter circumstances began to unfold: he had lost his job and had almost no money for Christmas— only a couple of dollars with which to purchase a few groceries for Christmas dinner. His funds were insufficient for anything but bare essentials.

The man with the turkey sized up the situation and realized he had the solution to both of their problems. He could unload the turkey in a way that was mutually beneficial. His first thought was to give it away; his second was to sell it for the few dollars, thinking that his new friend could salvage his dignity by paying for the meal.

And so he proposed the sale, explaining his dilemma and his resolution of it. The other man was elated, the exchange was made and the bird was taken home to wife and kiddies, who presumably gathered excitedly around the table while the turkey was unwrapped, only to discover that the bird their father had bought was a fraud.

You can imagine the disappointment and indignation of the defrauded family. The well-meaning turkey vender, however, went home satisfied that he had done a good deed for the day. I'm told that when he returned to work after the holidays and learned what his associates had done, he devoted most of his free time for the next month trying to track down the victim of his unintended scam, but he never saw the man again.

The offended family must believe to this day they were the victims of a cruel hoax—a classic example of man's inhumanity to man—but they would be wrong. The man's intentions were wholly good.

"Judge nothing before the appointed time," warns Paul. "Wait till the Lord comes. He will bring to light what is hidden in darkness and will expose the motives of men's hearts. At that time each will receive his praise from God."

Judgment is presumptuous on my part: only God knows the heart. And it's premature: I must wait until Jesus comes. He then will "bring to light what is hidden in darkness and expose the motives of men's hearts."

Time and God will give final judgment. Until then I must wait.

14

TOTAL CONTROL

"Beating my wings, all ways, within your cage I flutter, but not out."

—C. S. Lewis

NOW LISTEN, YOU WHO SAY, "TODAY OR TOMORROW WE WILL GO TO THIS or that city, spend a year there, carry on business and make money." Why, you do not even know what will happen tomorrow. What is your life? You are a mist that appears for a little while and then vanishes. Instead, you ought to say, "If it is the Lord's will, we will live and do this or that." As it is, you boast and brag. All such boasting is evil. Anyone, then, who knows the good he ought to do and doesn't do it, sins (James 4:13-17).

Planning is something we do every day, a necessary effort to make the most of our time here on earth. Without an intelligent plan, disorder and chaos overwhelm us.

Yet James insists that planning can be "evil" (his word, not mine) if we plan without making room for God. Why? Because it's presumptuous to assume that we have that much control over our lives. How can we presume to mark our calendars one year hence when we don't know what the next moment will bring? How can we plan so confidently for tomorrow when we may not be here when it comes?

You are a mist, says James, a vapor, a puff of smoke, a flitting cloud, a breath ("breath and britches," my Mother used to say). Here today, gone tomorrow. A vagrant virus, an inadvertent stumble, a stray bullet, an errant motorist strikes us down, or takes us out. We're completely at the mercy of our circumstances.

Yet circumstance is not chance. There are no random happenings, no uncaused events. The various fortunes of life are in God's hands. That's why we ought to say, "If the Lord wills I will do this or that." Anything else is playing God.

Here James is concerned with what theologians call Providence. The term comes from two Latin words *pro* and *videre*, meaning, "to look ahead" and thus "to plan in advance," and finally, "to carry out the plan." And since the agent of Providence is an all–knowing, all–powerful God whom nothing and no one can resist, literally *everything* is included in his plan.

I'm amused by an exchange in *Sleeper* in which Woody Allen is asked if he believes in God. "I'm a teleological, existential agnostic," Allen replies, "I believe there's an intelligence that governs the universe—with the exception of certain parts of New Jersey." Amused because Allen aptly expresses the popular theology of even Christians. We believe in the sovereignty of God—with the exception of certain parts of our lives. When it comes down to it, we're not sure if anyone is in complete control.

Yet in truth there can be no cause other than God. His wisdom is the reason for everything and his power the means by which everything is carried out. There are no accidents, no flukes, no fortuities, no maverick molecules, no loose ends. "There is no neutral ground in the universe," C. S. Lewis says. "Every square inch, every split second is claimed by God."

If you have trouble with this assertion I suggest you simply read the scriptures and let them make their own impression on you. (Take for example Psalm 139 and David's insistence that everything about him had been worked out in God's mind long before it was worked into his DNA.) You'll find that the writers express the thought of God's sovereignty repeatedly and incisively, but the assurance with which they express it, or simply assume it, should have an even more convincing effect.

The biblical writers were not fools. They saw the problem inherent in God's sovereignty and human free will. They understood they were dealing with issues that appeared to be conflicting and inexplicable, yet they did not stumble over apparent contradiction, nor did they try to reconcile what appear to be disparate facts. They simply asserted our moral responsibility in *all* things, and God's control over *all* things and moved on.

This is not the place to delve into this issue; it's enough to say at this point that there is no contradiction in God, only paradox and enigma. And the closer we get to our Lord the more paradoxical and enigmatic things begin to appear. We should expect that to be so. "If I knew of a theory in which was never an uncompleted arch or turret," George MacDonald wrote, "in whose circling wall was never a breach, that theory I should know but to avoid: such gaps are the eternal windows through which the dawn shall look in."

Infinite wisdom is something other than knowing more than finite beings; it is wisdom in another dimension and thus wisdom beyond our ken. All we can say is what the biblical writers so eloquently and explicitly say: despite our freedom, God is in *total* control. Beyond that we cannot go.

Naturally, if some god is substituted other than the God and Father of our Lord Jesus Christ this doctrine would be unspeakably cruel, but Providence is far more than *kismet* or impersonal, rigid control. Infinite love and wisdom lie behind every circumstance. If only we had eyes to see it, we would discover a loving and powerful Savior at work in every moment of our history and in every experience of our life—even in our sleep, our idle moments, and our play—turning us into glorious, winsome sons and daughters that he will enjoy forever.

Paul puts it this way: "We know that in all things (and he does mean *all* things) God works for the good of those who love him, who have been called according to his purpose. For those whom God foreknew he also predestined to be conformed to the likeness of his Son…"(Romans 8:28,29).

Paul is not suggesting that all things are good, or ought to feel good, but that all things are working for *our* good, the good for which we were created—to be just like God's own dear Son.

So, must we forego all planning and simply go with the flow? No, we can make our plans and dream our dreams, but we must do so fully aware of God's kindly and purposeful control. We "live and do this or that" as *he* wills and works out his durable, eternal purpose for us.

My friend Jim Catlin, recently wrote to me about a friend of his who had his life well mapped out, "I had to say to him," Jim wrote, "that life is seldom that linear, that predictable, and in light of God's sovereign plans for us, that discernible. We have an obligation, no a privilege, of exercising any capacity that God has given us to plan ahead, but ultimately we must give a nod of sovereignty to the One who *sees* the road ahead."

"If God wills," then, is not a shibboleth, or a pious cliché that we utter over our plans, but rather an attitude that pervades every aspect of our thoughts and schedules. It's a matter of knowing that we are in God's hands no matter what happens, recognizing that each event, circumstance, person, obstacle, intrusion that comes our way comes solely because God has willed it. It is accepting his will, saying "Amen" to the choices of the one who seeks our highest good, and in whose mind every step (and stop) has been eternally conceived out of love.

We can and must plan and make preparations for each day, but we must do so with all options open, freely giving God the right to revise, or revoke our plans according to his own will. The path he chooses for us may not be the one we would choose—the easier, gentler, less demanding path—but each situation has been scheduled from eternity to enable us make the most of our lives.

Furthermore, each situation, no matter how disturbing, has been screened through God's wisdom and love. Nothing is accidental or happenstance; everything has been planned in the eternal mind of a good and faithful Father who determines all things for our good.

I find contentment in that assurance. God's will is my safety—to know that I'm not on my own, to know that no matter what I plan I am *always* in God's plans. I can cast all my anxiety on him because he is caring for me.

To quote that peaceful angler, Isaac Walton: "When I would beget content and increase confidence in the providence of Almighty God, I will walk the meadows by some gliding stream, and there contemplate the lilies and other little dumb creatures for which God plans and cares *and therefore trust in Him.*"

The word "trust," they tell me, is an old contraction of the superlative degree of "true" (true, truer, *truest*). Trust knows that God is incomparably true when he tells us that all things—even those things that seem wrong or regressive—are determined for our ultimate, eternal good.

Are there deep disappointments in your life—unrelieved heartache over a dysfunctional family, an unfaithful spouse, a lost love, a lonely dark period that hides the face of God and obscures his love? The question is this, how do you regard these happenings? Have you grown resentful against them and against God? Are you frustrated because your plans have gone awry? Are you full of bitterness and cynicism because you think some blind fury is against you?

There is a better way—the way God's humble saints have always gone. It is to acknowledge God in all your ways, to know that Wisdom is at work though it may not seem to be working at all, quietly, invisibly, inexorably working all things for good. In this you can rest.

Thy will, not mine, O LORD,
However dark it be!
Lead me by Thine own hand,
Choose out the path for me.

Smooth let it be or rough,
It will be still the best;
Winding or straight, it leads
Right onward to Thy rest.

I dare not choose my lot;
I would not, if I might;
Choose Thou for me, my God;
So shall I walk aright.

Take Thou my cup, and it
With joy or sorrow fill,
As best to Thee may seem;
Choose Thou my good and ill.

Choose Thou for me my friends,
My sickness or my health;

Choose Thou my cares for me,
My poverty or wealth.

Not mine, not mine the choice,
In things or great or small;
Be Thou my Lord, my Love,
My Wisdom, and my All!

—Horatio Bonar

15

COMEUPPANCE

Though the mills of God grind slowly,
Yet they grind exceeding small
Though with patience he stands waiting,
With exactness grinds he all.

—Friedrich Von Logou

NOW LISTEN, YOU RICH PEOPLE, WEEP AND WAIL BECAUSE OF THE MISERY that is coming upon you. Your wealth has rotted, and moths have eaten your clothes. Your gold and silver are corroded. Their corrosion will testify against you and eat your flesh like fire. You have hoarded wealth in the last days. Look! The wages you failed to pay the workmen who mowed your fields are crying out against you. The cries of the harvesters have reached the ears of the Lord Almighty. You have lived on earth in luxury and self-indulgence. You have fattened yourselves in the day of slaughter. You have condemned and murdered innocent men, who were not opposing you (James 5:1-6).

. . .

Money and misery often go hand in hand, especially when money has been gained by exploiting others. Dishonest, ill–gotten riches riddle the soul with corruption; unprincipled men and women are ruined by the mold and decay that corrodes their wealth. "What is with the treasure fares as the treasure...The heart which haunts the treasure house where the moth and rust corrupt, will be exposed to the same ravages as the treasure... Many a man, many a woman, fair and flourishing to see, is going about with a rusty moth–eaten heart within the form of strength or beauty" (George MacDonald).

God sees the heart driven by ambition and greed, and some day those who enrich themselves by fraud and oppression will see it and feel it as well. The corruption of your souls and substance, says James, "will testify against you and eat your flesh like fire."

"You have hoarded wealth in the last days," warns James. Time is running out. The end of all things is at hand. "The cries of the (defrauded) harvesters have reached the ears of the Lord Almighty." Will not the Judge of all the earth do what is right? (Genesis 18:25).

"You have lived on earth in luxury and self-indulgence." You've had your day, but God's day is coming! "You have fattened yourselves in the day of slaughter"—like a pig, standing with both feet in the trough, fattening itself for the slaughterhouse, eating itself to death: one day there will be a reckoning.

Judgment is an enfeebled word in these days of unbridled tolerance, especially when it's applied to God. We prefer to think of a deity who lets bygones be bygones, who happily winks at wickedness, who says, "boys will be boys," and pats us on the back to build our self-esteem.

But God is just and ultimately must put an end to injustice. When we have become evil our doom is not long delayed. He will wait patiently for as long as it takes for a man or woman to repent and turn to him, for he is not willing that any should perish. But if there is no turning there is no escaping him. "God has feet of wool and hands of steel," runs an old Arab proverb, leaving us to draw our own conclusions.

Actually, no one has to tell us that judgment is looming. Every sane person knows it. Years ago I saw a segment on that wonderfully creative, satirical television program, *That Was The Week That Was* (otherwise known as *TW³*). In one brief scene David Frost sat behind a desk with two doors behind his back, one marked "Heaven," the other marked "Hell." A man approached the desk with his hat in his hands and asked, "Which way do I go?" Frost answered, "You know." The question and answer were repeated a number of times, then the man crumpled his hat and walked through the door marked "Hell." No one has to tell us. We know.

It seems to me, however, that James is not writing primarily to warn oppressors of imminent judgment. No, he's addressing oppressors for the sake of the oppressed. "The cries of the harvesters have reached the ears of the Lord Almighty," he assures them. God is standing at the door. His "coming is near" (5:8).

The cries of the oppressed have reached the ears of God Almighty and he will come in his own time to avenge his own. The wicked will be swept away; the world will be compelled to admit that there is a "God that judges in the earth" (Psalm 58:11). "Your suffering will not go on forever," he assures the oppressed. "There will be an end."

That being true, James issues unexpected and startling counsel: "Do not resist." That, I believe, is the force of his final statement, "You have condemned and murdered righteous men; *he does not resist you*."

Greek scholar Henry Alford paraphrases James' comment this way, "The behavior of the righteous under your persecution is ever that of meekness and submission." James' comment, thus, is more than an observation. It has the force of an assumption: righteous men and women do not resist evil.

James seems to be echoing Jesus words, "I tell you, do not resist an evil person. If someone strikes you on the right cheek, turn to him the other also" (Matthew 5:39). Righteous men and women do not retaliate and avenge themselves. They leave room for the wrath of God. Some people *need* to be repaid, but don't you do it. God treads the winepress of wrath and retribution *alone* (Isaiah 63:3).

Jesus put it another way, "Every plant, which my heavenly Father has not planted, will be rooted up. *Let them alone!*" (Matthew 15:13,14).

Some people are worthy of judgment, but the problem is that we're not wise enough to know when to seek revenge. The matter is far too complex for us; we don't know who to hurt and when to hurt them if we were to choose to. No, judgment is a job for God alone. He *alone* will establish righteousness on earth and establish it forever. The Judge of all earth will, in the end, do what is right.

The remarkable thing about our God, however, is that he may punish the wicked by placing their punishment on the cross. He may win them to himself because of the work of his Son. He may repay them with salvation. That is why we must "leave them alone."

In the meantime, we can take great comfort in the psalmist's words:

> Do not fret because of evil men, or be envious of those who do
> wrong; for like the grass they will soon wither, like green
> plants they will soon die away. Trust in the LORD and do good;
> dwell in the land and enjoy safe pasture. Delight yourself in
> the LORD and he will give you the desires of your heart.
> Commit your way to the LORD; trust in him and he will do
> this: He will make your righteousness shine like the dawn, the
> justice of your cause like the noonday sun. Be still before the
> LORD and wait patiently for him; do not fret when men
> succeed in their ways, when they carry out their wicked
> schemes. Refrain from anger and turn from wrath; do not fret
> —it leads only to evil. For evil men will be cut off, but those

who hope in the LORD will inherit the land. A little while, and
the wicked will be no more; though you look for them, they
will not be found. But the meek will inherit the land and enjoy
great peace" (Psalm 37:1-11).

This psalm, from which Jesus took his beatitude, "Blessed are the
meek," may lie behind James' words as well. It counsels meekness in
the face of grave injustice. Meekness is the means by which we overcome the world.

Meekness is not weakness. It is "strength under control," as Ray
Stedman used to say. It is strong enough to refuse to retaliate against
those who wrong us. It is great enough to be quiet, peaceful, and
unassuming in the face of grave injustice.

Remember Peter's words, "Christ also suffered for you, leaving you
an example for you to follow in His steps, who…while suffering,
uttered no threats, but kept entrusting himself to Him who judges
righteously" (I Peter 2:20–23). Jesus did not repay the world's cruelty.
He waited for the Father to defend him.

One church Father, Justin Martyr said, "Jesus' greatest miracle is that
he did not retaliate." When our Lord was stretched out on the cross,
instead of bitter recrimination he offered up his life to God and
waited for *his* vindication. That was the secret of his composure and
ours.

But, you say, is it wrong to redress injustice when it comes? It
depends. If we perceive injustice directed at another we must take
up their cause and do what we can to defend them. Love demands it.
Certainly, no decent person would stand by while another human
being was abused, battered or defrauded in some way.

Likewise, it may be necessary to defend ourselves on occasion. It was
Augustine, I think, who first pointed out that when Jesus taught us
to "turn the other cheek," he referred to the *right* cheek that was
struck (Matthew 5:38,39). Assuming that most assailants are right

handed and would therefore normally strike us on the left cheek, Jesus was not thinking of an assault, but an insult—a back–hand slap. In such cases we should, in deep humility, offer the other cheek.

No, I don't think James is saying we must never respond to injustice. He rather was concerned with the attitude in which we respond to oppression. His word, "oppose" is a strong word, meaning in some contexts, "to range in battle against." It has to do with all–out war and the rage and animosity that accompany it. For us to engage our oppressors in that spirit is to become like them. There is an old Quaker saying, "If we fight the beast by becoming a beast then bestiality has won."

So much depends on the spirit in which we oppose injustice. As Paul puts it, "The Lord's bond-servant must not be quarrelsome, but be kind to all, able to teach, patient when wronged" (2 Timothy 2:24, NASB). It's important that we show love, patience and kindness to all adversaries, even when we must speak out against them. Angry, bitter advocates do great harm.

And finally, when we have done all we can do, we must wait patiently until God avenges the wrong and vindicates us. He will set everything right—in this life or in the next. He is the Alpha and Omega; he and not our opponents will have the last word.

God "loves justice" (Psalm 11:7). In his time and in his way he will set everything right. He stands between us and our enemies; he will not leave us in their hands. He acts firmly and no one can interfere. In the meantime, we are shadowed and sheltered under his wings. No one can hinder or harm us there.

God says insistently and strongly: "They will fight against you, but they will not overcome you, for I am with you and will rescue you" (Jeremiah 1:19). He does not say we will not be assaulted, belabored or disquieted. He says we will not be overcome. "Nothing in life is quite so exhilarating," Winston Churchill once chortled, "as being shot at without result."

Knowing that God has taken up our cause enables us to be tranquil and strong. The weak have to defend their dignity and rights. Those who are strengthened by God can yield. "Let your forbearance be evident to all," Paul writes, "The Lord is near" (Philippians 4:5).

St. John of the Cross says that those who are guarded by God have three distinguishing characteristics—tranquillity, gentleness, and strength. Anxiety, intensity, instability and pessimism plague us when we try to protect ourselves, but those who are shielded and strengthened by God share the calm and quiet nature of the one in whom they trust.

> *Careless seems the Great Avenger;*
> *History's pages but record*
> *One death grapple in the darkness*
> *'Twixt old systems and the Word.*
> *Truth forever on the scaffold,*
> *Wrong forever on the throne.*
> *But that scaffold sways the future,*
> *And behind the dim unknown*
> *Standeth God within the shadows*
> *Keeping watch upon His own.*

—James R. Lowell

16

GREAT HEART

Endurance is the crowning quality,
And patience all the passion of great hearts.

—James Russell Lowell

BE PATIENT, THEN, BROTHERS, UNTIL THE LORD'S COMING. SEE HOW THE farmer waits for the land to yield its valuable crop and how patient he is for the autumn and spring rains. You too, be patient and stand firm, because the Lord's coming is near. Don't grumble against each other, brothers, or you will be judged. The Judge is standing at the door! Brothers, as an example of patience in the face of suffering, take the prophets who spoke in the name of the Lord. As you know, we consider blessed those who have persevered. You have heard of Job's perseverance and have seen what the Lord finally brought about. The Lord is full of compassion and mercy (James 5:7-11).

Says James—we must bear with unfailing patience the spiteful attacks of malice. We must be patient and kind under provocation.

We must hold our tongue, be quiet, unruffled and composed when passing through a swarm of unkindness and misrepresentation. We must try to right wrongs, not by force, but by patient dialogue and by the peaceful means our Lord employed. This is James' way—for those whose hearts are guarded by Jesus' sure promise, "I am coming back for you!" (John 14:28).

Patience is a necessary corollary of Christ's coming. Why should we not endure indignity and injustice in the face of ultimate and absolute justice? Is there any better hope than to know that Jesus is coming again to set all things right? Is there any better way to beget habits of patience and peace?

Like the farmer we put our trust in due process. The farmer plants the seed and waits patiently until the harvest appears. He's not disappointed or deterred by delay. We, likewise, await the process by which God will eradicate evil and gather up his own. He has given us his word that's he's coming back and put it in writing. It's the surest thing in the world. As Helmut Thieleke replied, when asked what he will say to Jesus at his appearing, "I knew you meant it."

The good life is a bonus, not something we're due. Unrelieved suffering and oppression may well be our lot here on earth. But here and here alone do we suffer for Jesus' sake. Though circumstances may seem bleak and hopeless at present, there's a better day coming —"a budding morrow at midnight," said Keats. Beyond the world of sight there is a judge, keeping watch over his own, waiting to answer every plea and avenge every wrong. God hates injustice and will vindicate us in due time.

In the meantime, when wrong inflicts us we should avoid vindicating ourselves. We may answer injustice as Nehemiah did and calmly state our case, but we must avoid vengeance and retaliation. That's a job for God.

We must be quiet unless our goal is the good of our detractor. We must turn instantly to our righteous judge asking him to vindicate the right and right the wrong. The weaker and more vulnerable we are the more thoroughly God can protect us.

We must not "grumble against one another," when afflicted. We must not blame our troubles on one another, which we're inclined to do when the real cause of our misfortune is inaccessible to us. Rather we should let our "sweet reasonableness" be known to all—even in the midst of intimidation and fear.

God wants to work in us those things that are unnatural for us. Anyone can be patient when everything's going his or her way. The greater thing is to be quiet and calm when circumstances are adverse.

Perhaps God has called you to endure being poorly served. Suffer it gladly, for this is acceptable to God. Learn to be patient, kind, and gentle in the midst of all that disturbs you. If you wrong others with an angry word, ask their forgiveness and do them some small act of kindness. Don't be discouraged by your mistakes, but continually come back to God.

Every day is full of disturbances. We must learn to deal with them. Each troublesome event teaches us to live patiently in the presence of God. We must not trust our good intentions, but seek his grace to be humble, tranquil and strong. He is accessible to all that want him. He stands just outside the door.

Everything, of course, takes time, and time is something God has plenty of. He has so much of it, in fact, that it's irrelevant: a day is as a thousand years to him and a thousand years as a day. That's why his timing seems so terrible at times. Like the exasperated psalmist, we cry out, "How long, O Lord? How long?"

But we must not hurry God unduly lest we force him to forego his best work. Delay is his primary tool for soul–making and especially for developing that quality we find hardest to achieve—patience. When we try to hurry God along we miss this.

As children we associated patience with passivity and inactivity, with those days when we were waiting for something that never seemed to come—a birthday, Christmas, a trip to Disneyland. We were told over and over again, "Be patient."

We struggled with helplessness. The only thing we could do is remain in our place while time marched on. Time was the tyrant; the hands on the clock ticking off the long minutes until we could open our presents, or get to the beach. With such memories, patience easily becomes pejorative.

But true patience is something more. It is a humble acceptance of God's ways while he works out his will for us. It is a calm assurance that Wisdom can make no mistakes and is doing all things well. It is a quiet confidence that "the Lord is full of compassion and mercy," and that someday we, like Job, will see what he has "*finally*[1] brought about."

> *One day at a time to be patient and strong,*
> *To be calm under trial and sweet under wrong,*
> *Then it's toiling shall pass and its sorrow shall cease;*
> *It shall darken and die; and our God will bring peace.*

—Annie Flint Johnson

17

TO RING TRUE

"I would like to ring true."

—G. K. Chesterton

"ABOVE ALL, MY BROTHERS, DO NOT SWEAR—NOT BY HEAVEN OR BY earth or by anything else. Let your 'Yes' be yes, and your 'No,' no, or you will be condemned" (James 5:12).

Honesty is the best policy, we say. No, honesty is the *only* policy, or so James would have us believe. "As for *you*," he writes, "let your 'Yes' be 'Yes' and your 'No' be 'No.'"

We must be true, so true there's no reason to swear by heaven, or earth, or the hair of our chinny, chin, chin; so true that a simple, quiet assertion will do. As John Stott said, "When a monosyllable will do, why waste your breath by adding to it."

James clearly had Jesus' words in mind: "You have heard that it was said to the people long ago, 'Do not break your oath, but keep the oaths you have made to the Lord.' But I tell you, do not swear at all: either by heaven, for it is God's throne; or by the earth, for it is his footstool; or by Jerusalem, for it is the city of the Great King. And do not swear by your head, for you cannot make even one hair white or black. Simply let your 'Yes' be 'Yes' and your 'No' be 'No'; anything beyond this comes from the evil one" (Matthew 5:33-37).

"Swearing" is not blasphemy and cursing, but oath–taking, a common practice in James' day. People took solemn pledges to assure others they were on the level, that what they were about to say was true, or what they said they would do, would get done.

There's nothing wrong with oaths as such. Even God has taken an oath on occasion (Genesis 22:6; Hebrews 6:13–18), though he has done so, not to increase his credibility, but to elicit and confirm our faith. The fault that made God condescend to this level is not his, but ours. Given the fact that the world is chock full of liars, we may wonder at times if even God is telling us the truth.

What James is saying is that honest men and women don't need to resort to oaths, not that they should refuse oaths when required to do so by an outside authority. Swearing is a tacit confession of human dishonesty and is essential in a world where men and women can't always be trusted. "Oaths arise because men are so often liars," A. M. Hunter said. It seems to me that love demands that we accommodate ourselves to the practice when required by law, and to show obedience and courtesy to the state. "A man may swear when the Magistrate requireth, in a cause of faith and charity…" is the way the Anglican *Articles of the Christian Religion* put it.

In common parlance, however, there's no need to swear that we're true, or call on anyone to back up our word, for our character should guarantee our words. If we're true in heart, our word alone should suffice.

Why do we find it necessary to introduce promises with an oath? The only reason is that we think our own words won't be believed. But the more we resort to oaths the more we degrade language and our reputations.

No, we should be so true that our reputation precedes us. Our conversations should be so honest and our character so veracious that no one can doubt us. A simple word will do. That condition, James says, is "above all."

Charles Eliot, who was president of Harvard University in the early 1900s, once announced that he was thinking of dropping baseball as a sport at the school. When pressed for an explanation, he answered, "This year the team did well because one pitcher had a good curve ball. I understand that a curve ball is thrown with a deliberate attempt to deceive. Surely that is not an ability we want to foster at Harvard."

Right. Nor should it be fostered, or found among God's people. Deception, dishonesty, duplicity and other lying behaviors should never be named among us. We must be true, through and through—not only in our words, but also in all that we do. That's the virtue we call integrity.

"Integrity" comes from the same Latin root as "integer," and carries with it the idea of wholeness. (Jerome, in fact, in the Latin Vulgate, translates the Greek word "whole" with the Latin, *integer*.) A person of integrity, like a whole number, is whole, undivided, one piece of cloth.

Integrity means that our souls are integrated by the truth. There are no segments of our existence from which truth is excluded, no fudge factors, no hidden agendas, no secret chambers reserved for falsehood and misrepresentation. We are true *all the way through*.

Integrity means that the same core values, ideals and absolutes govern our lives in all their parts. It means that no part of our behavior is a lie. We do not behave one way in one setting and a different way in another. We are the same whether at home, or away; on the job, or on the road; in public where others can observe us, or in private where no one can see what we do—unlike John Bunyan's loquacious companion, Talkative, who was "best abroad; at home he is ugly." As Howard Hendricks has put it, "The test of integrity is how you behave when no one is watching."

It means that we tell our stories straight without hyperbole and exaggeration. It means that whatever we have said is absolutely true. If we have said, "The check is in the mail," then it must be on its way. If we have agreed to do a job, then we must do it, no matter what it costs us. If we have promised to pray for a friend in need then, by all means, we must pray. If we have vowed "to love, honor and cherish until death separates us," then we must stick the landing, in so far as it depends upon us. Integrity means being dependable and faithful. We can be trusted; people can count on us in all that we do and say. That's what it means to be true (*cf.* 2 Kings 22:7).

Some time ago I received the following comment from Jim Catlin, my afore–mentioned friend. He's a great story–teller and his observations are shrewd and on the mark.

A few nights ago Dorothy had come home with a stack of videos from the local rental place. I was feeling a little poorly, recovering from some recent shoulder surgery so she hoped that this would distract me from the pain for a bit. It was the TV series "Lonesome Dove" which was broadcast back in 1988 and which, at the time, captivated our imaginations with its vivid characters.

In the story, Capt. McCall agrees to the deathbed wish of his lifelong friend Gus McCrae to bury him in Texas. While enroute from Montana to Texas with his friend's body, he's confronted by the curious along the way about why he was doing this crazy thing. In one such encounter, the Captain, being a man of few words, simply looked his questioner in the eyes and slowly drawled, "I gave him my word."

A long pause follows as the two men's eyes examine one another when finally the stranger says, "Yes, I can see that you did." The Captain nods contentedly and turns away.

I loved the drama of the moment because it so captured the character of the Captain. Strangers could even see it. His words and his actions were one, the lifelong resolve of an old Texas Ranger who had had his belly full of the slimy, truth-shifting, spin-doctored excuses of the low–lifes that he had brought to justice through the years. "I gave him my word." And for Captain Woodrow McCall no more was needed!

"Dare to be true," wrote George Herbert, "nothing can need a lie; a fault which needs it most grows two thereby." One lie leads to another and then to ruin. Falseness, deceit, and other forms of living in the dark may work well in the beginning, but they contain within them the seeds of destruction. Jadis, C. S. Lewis' lying White Witch, had a sleigh that worked well as long as Narnia was in the icy grip of her Hundred Years of Winter, but when Aslan came and the snow began to melt, her sleigh then began to pull hard.

There comes a time when God steps in and our duplicity no longer works. We're found out and exposed; we fall into humiliation and shame. The wise man wrote, "The integrity of the upright guides them, but the unfaithful are destroyed by their duplicity" (Proverbs 11:3). That's what it means to "*fall* into judgment."

Actually, it's a good thing to be exposed by God, because if not, the end would be more catastrophic. Liars fall into the clutches of the evil one—the liar and father of lies. We begin to believe our own lies so that we can no longer distinguish between good and evil. We become hard and cynical. We love and respect no one, not even ourselves. We should be glad that God in his grace exposes us. There are far worse conditions than being found out.

There's no need to be untrue. There is a Word that enables us to discriminate—to know that A is right and B is wrong, A is better, B is worse, A is beautiful; B is ugly; a Word to inform every aspect of our taste and judgment; a Word that exposes our obfuscations, clever little sophistries and subtle ways of lying to others and to ourselves.

We must weave that Word into our lives so that all our parts are conformed, so that all we say and do is true. Until the word is formed in us there is little sincerity or honesty in us, but when it begins to shape our thoughts it makes us true to ourselves and to others. We can "walk before God in integrity of heart and uprightness" (1 Kings 9:4).

Once more we're called to be something more than we are, something more than we can be on our own. Yet it's not what we are today that matters, but what we want to be. Do you *want* to be true? Then you're of a mind with God and on your way. Once honesty reaches the will God can begin to make you real. Then you too will ring true.

> LORD, *who may dwell in your sanctuary?*
> *Who may live on your holy hill?*
>
> *He…who speaks the truth from his heart…*
> *who keeps his word even when it hurts!*

—Psalm 15:1–4

18

TWO TOGETHER

"At this, Christian was somewhat moved and putting to all his strength, he quickly got up with Faithful, and did also outrun him, so that the last was first. Then did Christian vaingloriously smile, because he had gotten the start of his brother but not taking good heed to his feet, he suddenly stumbled and fell, and could not rise again, until Faithful came up to help him. Then, I saw in my dream they went on very lovingly together: and had sweet discourse of all things that had happened in their pilgrimage."

—John Bunyan, *The Pilgrim's Progress*

Is any one of you in trouble? He should pray. Is anyone happy? Let him sing songs of praise. Is any one of you sick? He should call the elders of the church to pray over him and anoint him with oil in the name of the Lord. And the prayer offered in faith will make the sick person well; the Lord will raise him up. If he has sinned, he will be forgiven. Therefore confess your sins to each other and pray for each other so that you may be healed. The prayer of a righteous man is powerful and effective. Elijah was a man just like us. He prayed earnestly that it would not rain, and it did not rain on the land for three and a half years. Again he prayed, and the heavens gave rain, and the earth produced its crops (James 5:13-18).

James speaks to the many stages and moods of the pilgrimage and concludes with instructions on healing the sick. Assuming most translations of this paragraph, he ends on the wrong note, or so it seems to me.

It's incongruous that James would conclude his book with instructions on healing the body when his preoccupation throughout has been with the health and welfare of our souls. Though I do believe God heals, I believe he's concerned in this text, not with physical illness, but with the *soul*–sickness that so frequently attends our pilgrimage. Let me explain.

The word "sick" in verse 13 actually means, "helpless" or "impotent," and though it's often used in the Gospels and Acts to refer to physical weakness, in the Epistles it almost always refers to *spiritual* limitation and disability. The context of James suggests the latter meaning.

The word "sick" appears again in verse 15: "The prayer offered in faith will restore the one who is *sick*." Here a different Greek word occurs that suggests "weariness" and "fatigue." It's found in only one other place in the New Testament: "Consider him who endured such opposition from sinful men, so that you will not *grow weary* and lose heart…" (Hebrews 12:3,4).

I understand James' text, then, as a word of encouragement to those who have been decimated by sin—who have tasted habitual defeat and have become discouraged in their struggle against besetting sins. He's concerned with the deep, penetrating pain that overwhelms us when we find ourselves in the grip of sinful habits, passions and obsessive behaviors from which we find it difficult, if not impossible, to escape. We're beat; we're sunk; we've had it.

James assures us that we need not soldier on alone. We can call for the elders—mature fellow-travelers—and ask for their prayers. Their intercessions, James assures us, will rekindle our weary spirits and renew our desire to press on. God himself, who refreshes us with his forgiving presence, will "raise (us) up" from despair and gloom, and thus "the prayer of faith" will bring about our healing. There will be an end to sin's domination.

helps
to
talk
share

The "anointing"? Just a gentle reminder that our Lord Jesus, the Spirit of Holiness (whose presence is aptly symbolized by medicinal oil) is the one who heals us and makes us holy. There is a balm in Gilead to heal the sin–sick soul.

Some sins are too much for us. We cannot deal with them alone, but need the efforts of other, more mature believers to help us gain release from Satan who has taken us captive to do his will. To struggle alone is to wither and die.

Martin Luther wrote, "No man should be alone when he opposes Satan. The church was instituted for this purpose, that hands may be joined together and one may help another. If the prayer of one doesn't help, the prayer of another will."

"Therefore," James concludes, "confess your sins to *each other* and pray for *each other* so that you may be healed. The prayer of a righteous man is powerful and effective."

It seems odd that James would move from calling for the elders to calling for grass–roots help, but I believe he's thinking here of *preventative* maintenance. We don't have to wait until evil overwhelms us and extreme measures become necessary. We can get help right now.

We can find a soul–mate, a trusted ally who will stand with us in our battle against sin, a kind and gentle friend who will listen to our deepest motivations, jealousies, frustrations and inclinations without judgment and censure, a caring presence, a loyal confidant to whom we can say without reservation, "This is the truth about me." Someone who will gently ask us about our secret thoughts, our darkest passions, our unobserved and unguarded moments—and then ask us if we have lied.

"Two are better than one," says the philosopher, "because they have a good return for their work: If one falls down, his friend can help him up. But pity the man who falls and has no one to help him up! (Ecclesiastes 4:9,10). As Dietrich Bonhoeffer said, "Confession is not a divine law, but an offer of divine help for the sinner."

Prayer is a primary factor in this fellowship. We cannot fix others; we cannot change them; we cannot really help them. We can only take them to our Great High Priest, who alone, "gives help in time of need" (Hebrews 4:16).

Prayer, in the sense that it brings us to God, is "powerful and effective." It is therapeutic; it heals! It is as God has promised—not that he will put an end to every physical affliction, but that he will put an end to sin. This he will do in his good time, and as surely as his own good name.

It seems a small thing to merely pray. Isn't there something else we must do? Indeed, but nothing essential. Prayer is the thing we must do before anything else is done. Remember Jesus' words, "Satan has desired to sift you like wheat, Peter, *but I have prayed for you.*"

Elijah, James reminds us, "was a man just like us"—an ordinary man —yet he accomplished extraordinary things through prayer. He changed the course of nature! Thus, when we pray for sin's cure something beyond us will be done: sinners will be *healed*," says James, using a verb tense that suggests "a *state* of healing." God will flow through our prayers to beget spiritual health and wholeness.

"Where there are so many all speech becomes a debate without end," wrote J. R. R. Tolkien, "but two together will find wisdom." This also is the promise of God.

19

LAST WORDS

"I will not give you counsel, saying do this or do that.
For not in doing, or in contriving, nor in choosing between this
course and another, can I avail, but only in knowing what was,
or is, and in part also what shall be."

—J. R. R. Tolkien

MY BROTHERS, IF ONE OF YOU SHOULD WANDER FROM THE TRUTH AND someone should bring him back, remember this: Whoever turns a sinner from the error of his way will save him from death and cover over a multitude of sins (James 5:19-20).

"Last words are lasting words," someone has said. So James leaves us with a final, enduring word of encouragement—to seek and save those that through perpetual yielding to sin have surrendered to it and wandered away from the truth.

This is the "sinner" of which James writes, the lost soul we must not dismiss or discard. We must seek and save him from death—that death–like state that enshrouds those who have given in to their shame.

"Death" is the slavery, frustration, confusion, and overwhelming sadness that inevitably follows resistance to God's will. It's what another generation of Christians would have called *acedia*—spiritual torpor and apathy, a "weariness of effort that extends to the heart and becomes a weariness of caring" (Melvin Maddocks).

James echoes Paul's words, "We urge you, brothers...encourage the weary, help the weak, be patient with all" (1 Thessalonians 5:14). God forbid that in the pursuit of our own holiness we should leave others behind.

At first, however, we don't need to say much to those who have fallen away. Certainly, we don't need to chide them. They know. "When one has the least thing on his conscience," said Kierkegaard, "he is immediately conscious of the infinite weight of God."

Fenelon, a 17th century saint wrote with great wisdom:

> Those who correct others should watch for the Holy Spirit to go ahead of them and touch a person's heart. Learn to imitate Him who reproves gently. People do not need to see God condemning them, they must realize within themselves that they have done something wrong. Do not be heavy–handed lest people see God as a judgmental ogre. When you become outraged over a person's fault, it is generally not righteous indignation but your own impatient personality expressing itself. Here is the imperfect pointing a finger at the imperfect. The more you selfishly love yourself, the more critical you will be. Self-love cannot forgive the self-love it discovers in others. Nothing is so offensive to a haughty, conceited heart as the sight of another one.

God's love is full of consideration, patience, and tenderness. It leads people out of their weakness and sin over time. It's better, then, to wait a long time before giving advice and correction and to listen long enough to know the sinner's heart. Reality rarely lies on the surface, but is found deep within. If we wait long enough we'll discern it.

If we'll just quell our compulsion to talk, if we'll be silent, wait, watch and pray until our friends are sure of us, we will begin to hear the pathos and misery in their souls, and then, as I have said, we cannot but speak in pity.

How often do I jump to conclusions about other's sins and begin to moralize without sensitivity and understanding? How often do I fail to feel my own sins as I hear theirs? How often do I speak without pity or compassion because I do not have the patience to hear someone out? How often do I *think* I know and yet do not know the inner person, never enter that sanctuary? Consequently, my words have no weight at all.

Consent must be gained by understanding, compassion and love. Until others know our love no words will do—not even God's word. Paul put it this way, "The Lord's servant must...be kind to everyone... He must gently instruct, in the hope that God will grant repentance leading to a knowledge of the truth" (2 Timothy 2:23–25).

Those enslaved by sin are victims of the evil one, who has taken them captive to do his will. If they are to be won at all they will be won by those who speak deeply and convincingly through love.

"Gently instructing" does suggest action. There is a time to speak, to help others feel their contamination and deal with it. Sin is elusive; we all have our fudge factors and loopholes. If we love one another we'll bring sin into the light rather than stand by while it works its harm on others. It's painful to confront others, but it's the loving thing to do. Faithful friends will wound if they must (Proverbs 27:6).

A true friend, Ambrose Bierce once observed, is one who stabs you in the *front!*

The issue is accountability: I am my brother's keeper. I am responsible for others, to watch over them, to instruct them, to counsel them, to admonish and correct them, to be engaged with them in their struggle against sin, to help them see their defilement and deal with it, but I must do so in kindness and love.

Paul writes, "Brothers, if someone is trapped in a sin, you who are spiritual (i.e. relying on the Spirit of Christ) should restore him gently…" (Gal. 6:1).

We must learn to deal gently with the faults of others. We must learn to be lenient with minor offenses—love overlooks a multitude of sins —even while we maintain our firmness in essential matters. True firmness is gentle, humble and kind. "A sharp tongue, a proud heart, and an iron hand have no place in God's work" (Fenelon). We must uphold a godly standard but we must not uphold it in an ungodly manner. The wisdom from above may be stern at times, but it is always gentle and kind.

But, again, though loving rebuke is love's duty it has always seemed to me that the worst argument for repentance is to argue strenuously for it. No amount of debate can convince a man or woman until the time for truth has come. Far better to join them in their journey, if they will have you, and wait for God's time to speak. There are precious few who will sit with those who are struggling in sin, who will be a quiet, loving presence, who will help sinners bear their burden of sin and thus fulfill the Law of Christ (Galatians 6:2).

And then, when we do speak we must speak of God's mercy and grace, for that is every sinner's salvation; they must know that his loving–kindness is everlasting. It is grace that teaches us to obey.

"Nothing but infinite pity is sufficient for the infinite pathos of life," wrote Amy Charmichael. God understands human misery as no one else does. He knows those who have been trampled underfoot as children, bent and broken by abuse. He grieves with those who are bending under a load of rejection and shame. He pities those whose hopes and dreams have been reduced to a flicker (Isaiah 42:3). His understanding is infinite. It is this "kindness," that draws men and women to repentance (Romans 2:4).

God's love, James insists, "covers a *multitude* of sins." Because Love has paid the price, a multitude of sins—all the sins accumulated over a lifetime—have been put away forever. "A most comfortable passage of scripture is this," says Matthew Henry. "We learn hence that though our sins are many, even a multitude, yet they may be hid or pardoned…never to appear in judgment against us."

We must assure sinners that the most outrageous and oft–repeated sins are forgiven according to God's mercy and grace. They can never go so far that God will not have them again. They cannot drift beyond his love and care. There is always a way back with God. Beyond the bad news of our failure and frustration is grace—that incredible gift of God.

Grace means that God forgives us, no matter what we have done, are doing, or will ever do. It means that our sins are gone forever—replaced by Love. "To say that (grace) is free unmerited favor only expresses a little of its meaning. It is the unhindered, wondrous, boundless love of God poured out to us in an infinite variety of ways without stint or measure, not according to our deserving, but according to His measureless heart of love" (Hannah Whitall Smith).

Wilt Thou forgive that sin where begun,
Which was my sin, though it were done before?
Wilt Thou forgive that sin through which I run,
And do run still, though still I do deplore?
When Thou hast done, Thou hast not done,
For I have more.

Wilt Thou forgive that sin which I have won
Others to sin? and made my sin their door?
Wilt Thou forgive that sin which I did shun
A year or two, but wallowed in a score?
When Thou hast done, Thou hast not done,
For I have more.

I have a sin of fear, that when I have spun
My last thread, I shall perish on the shore;
But swear by Thy self, that at my death Thy Son
Shall shine as he shines now and heretofore;
And, having done that, Thou hast done,-
I fear no more.

—John Donne

Grace also means that God has given us the resources to make a new beginning. The question is not, "Can I make it? Am I able? Can I overcome my sin? The question is always, "Is *he* able?" Can *he* transform me?" He says he can, though it may take awhile. God himself will sanctify us through and through. The one who calls us is faithful and he will do it (1 Thessalonians 5:24).

Sinners must start with God's part, with a calm assurance that grace for the next act of obedience is already there. They don't have to worry about tomorrow, or even this afternoon; they can move forward without fear or frustration knowing that the next step will take care of itself.

That's the good news—the gospel we must pass on to those who, through habitual failure, have fallen away. That's the gospel for *all* of us who have difficulty struggling upward into the light. That's the comfort we need to give to ourselves and to others.

Furthermore, we must assure those who have wandered away that God's love will *continue* to cover their sins, for many yearn to come home, but are afraid they will only fail again. We must assure them that God is never disappointed, nor is he surprised by human failure for it is inevitable. "It is a consoling idea," wrote Søren Kierkegaard, "that we are *always* in the wrong."

Long ago God made provision for our evil. Before we are born, before we did anything good or bad, our Lord paid for *all* our sins—those that were, those that are and those that shall be. Thus his love "covers a multitude of sins," even sin and guilt not yet acquired.

And in the meantime, despite false starts and failures, God is at work conforming some small part of all of us to his likeness, making us his portrait, his reproduction, his work of fine art. We can be confident of this: "He who began a good work in you will carry it on to completion until the day of Christ Jesus" (Philippians 1:6). God is never in a hurry, but he does mean business. He will finish the work as soon as he can.

This is the good news we must pass on to those who have given up and wandered away. This is the remedy to which we must resort for the correction of their sin.

Not all will receive it. Sin cleaves to individuals more or less, according the inclination they have for it. It's not sin as such that holds them, but the love of sin. If they do not want purity, they will not have it for God does not foist anything on those who do not want it. That would be neither kind nor wise.

But if sinners hate their sin, if their love of truth is pure and simple, if they are willing to turn toward the light, even if they've fallen into utter ruin, they can be thoroughly saved. It's not what they are, or what they have been that matters, but what they long to be.

And even if they struggle with besetting sin for a season—God's unsearchable wisdom for some—it cannot dominate them forever. They will learn humility, they will see progress in holiness, and though always in-process they will know the relief of full and final forgiveness. All sins are covered. Guilt, fear and pain are transmuted into happiness and joy—both theirs and ours.

And so James ends his book on this brief note, leaving us with this simple, sublime benediction ringing in our ears: "Whoever turns a sinner from the error of his way will save him from death and cover over a multitude of sins." This is the highest calling, the holiest healing.

One of George MacDonald's characters asks, "Havna everybody the care o' the others?" To save a soul from death, to turn another to righteousness, to help someone rise above sin and shame to become better, wiser, more like God—who could ask for anything more?

NOTES

EPIGRAPH

1. You can access David Roper's E-Musings at http://davidroper.blogspot.com/

5. WHY COMES TEMPTATION?

1. This is the same word James uses in verse 2 that is translated "trials." The New Testament employs the same word for both "trials" (adversity) and "temptation" (solicitation to sin). Context determines the meaning in each case.

6. THE LAW THAT SETS YOU FREE

1. The NASB has the better translation: "This (what he has written) you know, my beloved brethren. But let everyone be quick to hear, slow to speak and slow to anger…" (James 1:19).
2. "Quick to hear" is an old rabbinical saying: "Quick to hear and slow to forget; he is wise."

7. LITTLE THINGS MEAN A LOT

1. James uses a different verb in verse 22, that suggests *circumventing* the truth, but the essential idea is the same.

8. FRIENDS IN LOW PLACES

1. The form implies doubt as to the fact questioned.

9. FAITH THAT WORKS

1. Again, the grammatical form of the question anticipates a negative answer.
2. *Cf.* Ephesians 1:15; 3:17; 6:23; Colossians 1:4, 5; 1Thessalonians 1:3, 6; 2Thessalonians 1:3; 1Timothy 1:5; 1Timothy 1:14; 6:11.
3. The word translated, "tremble" actually means "to bristle up."

10. THE TELLTALE TONGUE

1. 2 Kings 1:2,3,16

11. GENTLE WISDOM

1. The text actually reads "Let him show forth his deeds in gentle wisdom."

12. WAR AND PEACE

1. The word is *hedone*.
2. I am indebted to classicist, Dr. William Barklay, for these texts.

16. GREAT HEART

1. The word refers to the end of all things.